On the Other Side

On the Other Side.

(African Americans Tell of Healing)

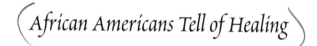

Alita Anderson

Westminster John Knox Press
LOUISVILLE
LONDON • LEIDEN

© 2001 Alita Anderson

Scripture quotations, unless otherwise indicated, are from the New Revised Standard Version of the Bible, copyright © 1989 by the Division of Christian Education of the National Council of the Churches of Christ in the U.S.A., and used by permission.

Illustrations are copyright © 2001 by Alita Anderson.

Bernice Johnson Reagon's "Preface to *Wade in the Water*" (introduction statement) is from Sweet Honey in the Rock: Live at Carnegie Hall, 1988, Flying Fish Records. Permission is granted by Bernice Johnson Reagon, copyright © Songtalk Publishing Co. (BMI).

Book design by Sharon Adams
Cover design by Terry Dugan Design
Cover illustration: The Baptism *by Alita Anderson, 1999. Acrylic on canvas, 11 × 14 in.*

First edition
Published by Westminster John Knox Press
Louisville, Kentucky

This book is printed on acid-free paper that meets the American National Standards Institute Z39.48 standard.

PRINTED IN THE UNITED STATES OF AMERICA

01 02 03 04 05 06 07 08 09 10 — 10 9 8 7 6 5 4 3 2 1

Library of Congress Cataloging-in-Publication Data

On the other side : African Americans tell of healing / [edited by] Alita Anderson ; illustrated by the author.
    p. cm.
    ISBN 0-664-22357-5 (pbk. : alk. paper)
    1. Spiritual healing—United States. 2. African Americans—Religion. I. Anderson, Alita, 1974–

BT732.5.O5 2001
234'.131'089960732—dc21

2001026901

When there is the promise of a storm
And you want change in your life
Walk into it.
If you get to the other side
You will be different.
—Bernice Johnson Reagon,
"Preface to *Wade in the Water*"

THE JOURNEY

A CKNOWLEDGMENTS

*T*he testimonies in this book are real. They are the real words of real people, which were tape recorded, transcribed, and slightly edited to preserve narrative flow. Most of the names, as well as the dates and places of origin, have been changed, because the testimonies in this book are personal. Those who shared their experiences opened portions of their lives in ways even those closest to them have not seen. The testimonies in this book are inspirational. In some way, they all give honor to God. This phenomenon was a revelation that evolved during the gathering process. I asked these wise ones to tell me about their experiences with healing. Expecting to hear solely stories of physical renewal, I was enlightened, for speakers also shared testimonies of spiritual and emotional transformation, transformations inextricably linked to their relationship with God.

Don't be confused. For these wise ones, healing is a process, not an end point. It is a process that you see evolving over the course of their testimonies, a process that can be celebrated even in the face of death.

I offer much gratitude to those who unselfishly opened their lives for the purposes of developing this book. Their desire is that we learn from their experiences. It is my prayer that when they see this work, they will know the honor that I felt to be the gatherer of their words. I promised Diva, one of the sharers, that I would mention somewhere in the book that mental illness affects the lives of many African Americans. The place to do that is here. She urges anyone who struggles with a mental illness to not be afraid to seek counseling.

There are those without whose encouragement this journey would not have been taken: Dean Gifford, Dean Andrien, Sally, Cordelle, Grandma and Grandpa, Aunt Linda, Jackie, and Canangela. Your words gave me the strength to step forward.

There are those who lifted me along the way: Gia, Kenya, Uncle George, Aunt Chee, Harley, Joya, Fadonna, Mil, Judy, Brian, and John. Your love moved me along.

There are those without whose generosity this work would not be available to your eyes: Dr. Gloria Wade-Gayles, Dr. Gail Bowman, Dr. Gilbert Bond, Dr. Ezra Griffith, Dr. Cariaga-Lo, and Michael Hobbs, Esq. Your assurance made the publishing of this work possible.

There are my parents who taught me to believe.

There is Larry who helped me to understand.

There is Westminster John Knox Press and Angela, my editor and friend, who received this stone and saw in it a jewel.

And ultimately there is God. Thank you, dear father, for these are truly the works of your hand.

WATERS

Wade in the water. Wade in the water, children.
Wade in the water. God's gonna trouble the water.

—Anon, "Wade in the Water"

I've been in the storm so long, children.
Oh give me a little time to pray.

—Anon, "I've Been in the Storm So Long"

Healing water over in Jordan.
How I long to see that day.

—Anon, "Gideon's Bank"

Waters run deep in the history of African Americans. The Atlantic's rugged ebb brought us to this land, and the Mississippi's flow freed us. Spirituals—the songs that are more than songs and were created by our ancestors—often speak of waters. They speak of "storms" and "wide rivers." They invite us to "sail the oceans" or "cross the chilly Jordan" to get to that "Promised Land" of freedom and peace.

The stories in this book are about wading waters. They speak of finding one's way out of the storm. While traveling with these tellers, you will undoubtedly find yourself laughing and crying or shouting aloud, as I have many times over, for these stories do more than remind us of our pain. They remind us that the promises of "that land," which we so long for, are ours to hold while here on earth. They invoke us to not only wade in the waters, but to know that triumph awaits us with her hands extended as we pass through.

In remembrance of those whose beacon voices lit our ancestors' paths to freedom, the verses of African-American spirituals are woven into the text of these oral narratives, guiding our storytellers along their own underground railroads. In this collection of oral testimonies are stories of faith. They are stories of perseverance and love. They are stories of healing that serve to remind all of us who have been in the storm too long to cross on over, for the "Other Side" is just a step away.

a.a., untitled, 2000. Acrylic on canvas, 8 x 10 in.

Journey deep and journey wide,
But I've got a home on the other side.

—Anon, "So Sad"

ALITA

I suppose it was her story that started the journey, told while we were sitting around the family room, hands deep in cornrowed hair. The television was on and the children were running while the pot of greens simmered on the stove. I don't remember how we got to it—maybe through talking about men, or maybe through talking about pain—likely a bit of both. But Victory, though well approaching seventy, was like a young girl when she spoke of Mississippi summers or falling in love. Victory had just married her young sweetheart, and a charming wife she was, all embracing of her new family, even the young favorite female cousin whom her husband insisted they house. They became the best of friends, she and her housemated-kin. But this was before Victory fell ill, before her body shut down on itself and Victory was restricted to her marriage bed—alone. The others became frightened when Victory didn't heal, and after awhile, only her mother remained.

Victory hadn't walked, she said, for months. Her mother sat on the dusky porch one mid-morning and looked sternly at the stranger when he approached. Taking off his hat and nodding with the gentility of those home trained, the stranger pointed at the door. "There is sickness in that house," he said. Victory's mother, wondering how this visitor arrived, replied quizzically, "Yes."

"I can heal her," he proclaimed.

And as desperate as she was discerning, Victory's mother let him in.

The stranger gathered the worn tin washbasin and filled it with warm water and the roots that he removed from his battered black jacket. After whirling the mixture with his prayer-chastened hands, he approached the bed and gently lifted Victory's body from its wed-locked chamber. He then placed her slowly in the basin and commanded her to walk. Feeble-limbed, Victory found her listless legs lifting themselves and sinking suddenly to the floor beneath. They steadied, and she, dripping with herbs and anointed water, stood. The stranger pointed again, this time to her bed, and told her to lift the mattress. Beneath it lay the bones of a black cat—the curse set by her housemated-kin—the favorite one who was in actuality her husband's mistress in disguise. That, Victory said, was the beginning of her healing.

It was after my second year of medical school at Yale that I began to feel the urge to leave. Frightened, I ignored it. Leaving was beyond the question for me, the one who carried the pride of my community and the hopes of my family in my arms. I was the first from my historically black college to enter that particular medical school; and feeling that I must succeed for those who wanted to come after me, leaving was not an option. But the urge knew nothing of obligations or options, and as time progressed it became insurmountable. So with a gentle pardon from an accepting dean and my promise to return, I went home.

Four months after leaving and wondering why I had forsaken face and career, I was sitting in silence when I remembered Victory's story. I remembered the tin washbasin, the pointed hand, and my vision of collecting other stories like hers to tell us how we heal. I suppose, looking back now, I can say that I was hurting, and that this journey was, in fact, my own to the other side. But that is hindsight's clarity. Then, I simply surrendered to the spirit greater than myself and allowed its gentle arms to carry me to each sage along the way.

a.a., *Kenny B,* 2001. Mixed media on canvas, 17 x 18 in.

O rise, shine, for thy light is a-comin'
Rise, shine, for thy light is a-comin'
Rise, shine, for thy light is a-comin'
My Lord says he's comin' by 'n' by.

This is the year of Jubilee
My Lord says he's comin' by 'n' by.
My Lord has set his people free
My Lord says he's comin' by 'n' by.

Intend to shout and never stop
My Lord says he's comin' by 'n' by.
Until I reach the mountain top
My Lord says he's comin' by 'n' by.

Wet or dry I 'ntend to try
My Lord says he's comin' by 'n' by.
To serve the Lord until I die
My Lord says he's comin' by 'n' by.

O rise, shine, for thy light is a-comin'
Rise, shine, for thy light is a-comin'
Rise, shine, for thy light is a-comin'
My Lord says he's comin' by 'n' by.

—Anon,
"Rise, Shine, for Thy Light Is Coming"

KENNY B

He was a legend, somewhat. I first heard of him in a tribute to the powers of wheat grass. He, who had lost fifty-six pounds last year, was the valedictorian of the health store in which I worked. Little did I know that in 1998 Kenny B let go of more than pounds.

Kenny would amble into the store with a smile as large as his three-hundred-pound body and a spirit that carried the morning sun. As he settled himself on the feeble stool, Kenny would wait patiently until my attention was his. Kenny always had a story that, whether it was about an "A" on an examination or a flat tire, began and ended with "I have been so blessed!" Listening to Kenny tell stories was as enchanting as watching a puppeteer, and because of this, the small store would quiet, and even those who were rushing out to work would slow their steps when he began.

I honestly don't know how long it was before I knew that Kenny had a testimony. Kenny would often mention, with no evidence of remorse, his AA (Alcoholics Anonymous) meetings and his divorce, but I bore them no mind because they, too, were wrapped in his cloak of sunshine. Yet I do remember that day when I, while wiping the counter, mentioned casually that I was seeking the stories of survivors, and Kenny's ever-bright countenance clouded. That, I do believe,

was the first time that Kenny looked into my eyes with gravity. Quietly he whis-
pered, "I have a story," and somehow I knew that this story was not Kenny's
daily yarn. Somehow I knew that this tale would be one of transcendence.

Later, we sat at the outdoor café, enveloped by the cool of evening. I fidgeted
with tape recorder in hand, trying to hide my nervousness while Kenny calmly
glanced over the menu. He was the first person to share his testimony with me,
and I wasn't quite sure of what to do. Maybe Kenny sensed my nervousness, or
maybe he too knew that this book was more of a pilgrimage than a project. What-
ever the reason, Kenny gracefully stretched his large hands over the small wob-
bly table and said, "Let's pray."

A calm fell over us that evening. The warm sun set. The waiters delivered
smoked salmon and cheesecake. The candles burned. And softly, above the sounds
of silverware and easy conversation, Kenny began.

> *Oh, I had so many fears, but he took them all away.*
>
> —Anon, "All the Way to Calvary"

I grew up in a household where there was a lot of fear. I had a very abusive stepfather. He used to do a lot of things to us. I was really afraid of him. He would
just holler and yell and say evil things to me. I remember him telling me, "Boy,
you ain't shit, and you ain't never gonna be shit." Yeah, he used to tell me that
all of the time. So I really grew up with a very poor self-image.

I remember that before I could tell time, I could feel when he was about to come home. If it was the summertime, I would hide under the porch. If it was the wintertime and it was too cold to be outside, I would actually go and hide under my bed just so I wouldn't have to face him. I grew up being afraid in my own house.

When I got to high school and started playing football, it seemed like my whole life changed. It seemed like for once in my life my stepfather was really proud of me. It seemed like for the first time in my life, I had some self-esteem, 'cause I was really good. The day I walked on the football field, they told me that I was going to play pro football.

By the time I got into college, I was an offensive tackle. I was the big man on campus. Nobody had a party without inviting me. I can remember an article coming out in the paper saying *"Kenny B: The Best Player in the Conference. He will definitely play pro football."* I had my picture in the paper, and I had girls coming at me. It was the happiest time in my life. I was strong. I was powerful.

My stepfather would come see me at those games. I felt good. It seems like during the period when I played football he was proud of me. He never would say it, though. But I was kinda proud of the fact that my parents would come up there every weekend to see us. I was real proud of that.

Up 'til this day, that period in my life was the happiest time. I looked forward to being a football player, and I was as strong as an ox. I was built like a brick house—you know what I mean. I was so developed that when I walked downtown the first thing that people would say to me was "Are you a football player?" If I would go into a supermarket, people would stare at me. They would turn and look and stare at me because that is how built I was. Physically, I was there. I was a specimen. People would actually walk up to me and feel my muscles. Yeah. People that I wouldn't know would do that sometimes. So I was real conceited.

This period in my life lasted all the way up to my junior year of college; then, all of a sudden, I started having double vision and I couldn't see. I went from being a really good football player to being a really bad one. When I tried to tackle people, I would see two of them, and I couldn't figure out who to hit or who to tackle. I got really weak, and I went from dominating people to being beat down by everybody. I didn't know what was going on.

Finally, they sent me to get my physical. They looked at my x-ray, and they thought that I had an enlarged heart. At the time, having an enlarged heart was really dangerous, so they sent me to a hospital in Houston. There they diagnosed me with this muscle disease called myasthenia gravis. At the time, I was twenty years old, and they told me that I wouldn't have but two years to live.

I didn't accept it. I really didn't accept it. It was like they told me that, and I told the doctor that it wasn't true. I couldn't accept it. I was convinced that the doctors didn't know what they were talking about. I was convinced of my invincibility. I didn't think nothing could hurt me. I didn't catch colds. I didn't get sick. I can remember being jumped on one time in a bar by five or six white guys, and I beat the hell out of them. You couldn't tell me nothin' at the time. I was taking my medicine, my myasthenia went into remission, and I went back to school to play football my senior year. I would have been drafted by the Cowboys that senior year, but the week that I was supposed to go to Dallas, I got sick with the myasthenia and had to go back home.

I saw the light.

> —Anon, "I Saw the Light"

I can remember being at home, sitting on the porch and feeling pretty weak one day, when my stepfather got home from work. He just took one look at me and called the ambulance. At that age, I didn't think that I could die. I could barely breathe, but it never occurred to me to call the ambulance. My stepfather saved my life.

The ambulance came, and as soon as I got to the hospital they hooked me up to a respirator. The guy that was working on the respirator stuck the tube down the wrong way, and my lungs started filling up with fluid. I almost died. I can remember coming up out of my body and looking down on the doctors. I can remember going up to the light, and when I got there, it was real peaceful and love. It was incredible. I didn't want to go back into my body, but because I heard the doctors calling my name, I went back. I came out of the light and I went back. I can remember coming back down through the ceiling and looking at the doctors. Then I went back into my body. I don't remember anything after that. The next day, I can remember the doctors saying over me, "We almost lost him last night." I was on respirators four or five times after that. I have almost died four or five times.

There's no hiding place down there.

> —Anon, "There's No Hiding Place Down There"

I started getting better, but then I would try to get work and I would get sick again. Every time it seemed like I was going to work and do good, I would get sick. I ended up losing jobs. I had to quit jobs, and I think it finally built up. I became an alcoholic. I went from being a very powerful man to having a muscle disease that made me very weak. My strength was me. It was my identity, and when I lost it, I lost myself. It took me about seven years to become a full-blown alcoholic. I went from drinking a six-pack a week to drinking a fifth of liquor every night.

To me, I was just depressed. I felt like a loser. The fear came back. I think that I have lived most of my life in fear. Fear that I was not going to make it. Fear that I was not going to live up. When I started losing all of the jobs, my step-father came back to me saying, "You ain't shit, and you ain't never gonna be shit." Instead of hiding under the bed I was hiding under the alcohol.

Finally, I started going to AA. I would get a year clean, then I would relapse. Get a year clean, then relapse. After a while, I just got tired of relapsing. I was lonely. I had blown up to three hundred seventy-five pounds, and I could barely walk. I would approach women, and they would be really nice to me, but I was sick, and they knew that I was sick. I couldn't get dates. I was miserable. It got to the point where all I could do was eat and look at TV.

People would pray for me, and I never got healed. But I remember 1998. At the end of 1998, my pastor asked me to come to watch-night service. I really didn't want to go. As you know, watch night is on New Year's Eve, and in the past, I would always go out and go to a club or something like that. I really didn't want to go to watch night that night, but I had promised, so I went.

Jubilee, Jubilee, Oh my Lord, Jubilee.

—Anon, "Jubilee"

My church is a small church of about forty people, and everybody was there that night. Right before midnight, my pastor got up and got to preaching about Jubilee. He was speaking about how the year of Jubilee was the year of restoration and how in the old days, even land that people had sold would come back to the family. People were let out of prison, debt was forgiven, and I just thought that concept sounded so spiritual. There was just something that seemed so right about it. People had prayed for me in the past. They had prayed for me, and I knew that I always wanted to be healed, but I never got healed. But that night, I started believing in the concept of restoration. That night, the pastor asked if anyone wanted to be restored, and I walked up to the altar. When I got up to the altar, I just felt a lot of peace and love, like that first time in the hospital when I almost died. I just felt a lot of peace and love. I believe that I actually heard God say, "You are going to be healed." I actually heard that. It wasn't an audible voice; it was talking to my spirit, and I just knew right then that I was going to be healed, and I was.

That night, I felt my fear leave. That night, I knew that God was going to take care of me, and my whole life changed. See, all of my life I had been stressing about being healed physically, but that night I was healed emotionally, and when I was healed emotionally, my body got better.

I was taking thirteen medications at the time—over twenty-something pills a day. I had diabetes. I had high blood pressure. I had chronic gout. In that first year, the diabetes left, the high blood pressure left, and I was losing weight. I lost fifty-six pounds in 1998. I was on Prozac for depression, and the depression went away. I stopped taking all of the medication. I started eating right, and I just started feeling better. I started getting strong.

I know that God has healed me. Now, I am walking. I lift weights. I work out every day. I got women approaching me. I am still fat. I still weigh over three hundred pounds. I still don't have a job that I would want to have, but I am happy. I wake up in the morning knowing that whatever happens, God is going to take care of me.

It is like I keep having miracles in my life. God just keeps surprising me. When I do the next right thing, God always takes care of me. When I stay in God's will, he always takes care of me. He has never failed. The only time that he didn't take care of me was when I didn't have faith in him, when I was taking control and trying to run things. That is when I always got in trouble. That watch-night service, the fear went away because I knew that God would take care of me. I really knew that, and He has continually blessed me.

Sometimes that fear tries to come back, but when it does, I just look it in the face and tell it to get behind me. I just don't stay where I used to stay. That is all about recovery. It is not about what happens; it is about how you respond to it. It really is.

Seeker, seeker, give up your heart to God.

—Anon, "The Rocks and the Mountain"

I did a talk on forgiveness once. I think of the insight and the revelations that brought me there. I have never heard anyone talk on forgiveness like I do. I taught that one part of forgiveness is accepting people for who they are. Accepting them with their character defects. I talked about how sometimes things happen in our life where we want to blame God, or we want to blame other folks, and we just have got to forgive them. People talk about predestination and free will, and I really don't want to get into that. It is a fact that when God says that something has got to happen, it happens. If people have a part that God has them to play in your life, then how can you be angry with them if they did what God has placed them to do? What I am saying is that it is for you. It is not really for the other person. The energy, the anger—I just know that when I gave up a lot of that—when I forgave my stepfather. . . .

When my stepfather died, his sister was telling me how their father used to beat them. How he would just strip them naked and beat them. Their father would just beat them for nothing. Then it dawned on me. My stepfather never would beat us. When I did something wrong, he would punish me. He would spank us sometimes, but he never beat us. And you know what? He would never let my mother do it either, especially if she was going to whip me in front of other kids. He would stop it. He never would allow it.

It dawned on me that in his own sick way, he was trying to do better. He did a lot of little sick things, but in his way, in his mind, he was honestly trying to do better than his father did to him. In his way he loved me, and in his way he was trying to show me his love. When I realized that, all of the resentment went away. Now when I think about him, tears come to my eyes because I really hated him for so long. But when I didn't have to hate him anymore, the weight of the world came off of my shoulders.

I don't get angry about other people's character defects anymore. I don't get angry with people for being who they are. I realize that I can't change people and how they feel. I can only change Kenny, and when I change Kenny, everything else changes. That was a lesson. I've been hearing that lesson for years, but it was never in the heart. See, what I have learned is, until you enter a life or death situation, you ain't gonna change. You are gonna keep on doing what you are doing. Until you have a spiritual awakening, until you let God change you, you cannot change. When I do what God wants for me to do, it works out. When I do the next right thing, it works out. I don't have to change it. God changes it.

That is what I am learning, and it is a victory every day. It is like being a little kid growing up. When you get a new truth, it just warms the spirit up. You know it's funny, because I am still a heavyweight and my eyes still look funny because I see two of everything, but life is fun for me now. I am having a good time. I am still growing up, and I am just excited.

Every day to me is an adventure. I am going to school in March to get a finance degree. I am real excited about that. A few years ago, that old fear would have come up and said, "You are going to start this job and you will get sick. You are going to go to school and you will get sick." Today I know that God is going to take care of me. I am going to go to school, and even if it takes me years, I am going to get up and go to school, even if I have to go in a wheelchair. I know that God is going to take care of me, and I know that I have got to do what I need to do. I know that I have been blessed. All of my life I have known that I have been blessed. It is just that now I have really started to realize it, appreciate it, to try to give it back, and be where God wants me to be in my life. When I do the next right thing, he will always take care of me.

By then, our forks rested on smudged plates, and the only sounds remaining were the Georgia night crickets and Ella Fitzgerald singing softly of love. It seemed that again Kenny had slowed and silenced the crowd.

As we got up to leave, I, swept in the wonder of Kenny's testimony, felt like an air-tossed child who knew that loving arms were below to break her fall. I thought of my own fears, my own front porches and under-bed spaces, and my own bottles that I used to hide from them. I thought of my own challenges of change and rested in remembering the power of forgiveness.

I admired this man who had lost his physical strength. I admired this man who had lost that which carried his identity, his sense of worth and success. Looking into his eyes, I knew that in the process he had gained a spiritual strength, faith, and insuppressible joy. Looking into his eyes, I knew that Kenny had healed and that his healing lay in the transformation.

I don't think I ever saw Kenny the same after that evening. Before, he was the jolly man who greeted my mornings with pleasant stories and an infectious smile.

After that evening of cheesecake and conversation, I realized that Kenny was much more. I realized that he was a champion over paralyzing fear and a victor in a lifelong battle for self-love. I realized that Kenny was a conqueror, and, in my mind, he would always be a legend.

a.a., *Girlchild*, 2000. Acrylic on canvas, 4.5 x 5.5 in.

hen the storm of life is raging
Stand by me.
When the storm of life is raging
Stand by me.
When the world is tossing me
Like a ship upon the sea,
Thou who rulest wind and water,
Stand by me.
Thou who rulest wind and water,
Stand by me!

In the midst of tribulation,
Stand by me.
When the hosts of hell assail me,
And my strength begins to fail me,
Thou who never lost a battle,
Stand by me,
Oh, stand by me.
Thou who never lost a battle,
Stand by me.

In the midst of faults and failures,
Stand by me.
When I do the best I can,
And my friends misunderstand,
Stand by me.
Thou who knowest all about me,
Stand by me,
Oh, stand by me,
Thou who knowest all about me,
Stand by me.

> — Anon, "Stand by Me"

IJOMA

(Ije-oma—Igbo (Nigeria), "safe journey")

I entered this journey with no idea of how I was to find the sharers. Somehow, I knew that they would come, and they did, each in their own way, each in their own time. And one came before I even knew that the book would be written.

Driving to her house felt like a familiar but haunting dream. Ijoma was a spiritualist whom I heard about through my friend, her client, Roxanne. Ijoma lived three mailboxes down from the house where my beloved grandmother lived and died. I hadn't been on that street since childhood, and when I reached Ijoma's front porch, overwhelmed with the clamor of not-too-distant memories, I considered forgoing the visit. Then the warmth of burning frankincense began its embrace. Ijoma's door creaked open, and there stood a woman as beautiful as a cypress against the evening sky. She had skin the color of roasted chestnuts and hair long and locked, which she wrapped around her head like woven ebony. But it was her eyes that I remembered. It was as if they saw, in the present moment, both my past and my future. They looked both ancient and innocent, both knowing and unknown.

I had seen them before, my memory reminded me. Some years ago, randomly at a fair, they looked up at me intently as I made pleasant conversation about her jewelry on display. She told me then that we would one day meet again. I remembered that incident now and stood paralyzed. Ijoma reached for my hand and led me in.

We moved around the bright and simple room, and as I got situated I wondered whose story Ijoma would share. I knew from Roxanne that Ijoma was a channel for many healings, and I was hoping that she would have a few interesting client stories. Yet when I asked Ijoma whose story she would be sharing, her ancient eyes lowered. After that, the shuffling ceased, for Ijoma said, "My own."

I always saw things as a child. I was always seeing flashes of light or faces or shadows moving about the room. When I would say to someone, "Did you see that face?" or "Did you see that man that just walked by?" they'd tell me, "No. There is no such thing!" I would hear footsteps a lot of times. I'd hear voices talking. Sometimes I would say I saw a ghost, and people would tell me that I was crazy. I just felt scared.

I was young when the spirit first spoke to me. I remember having my first conscious channeling—where I really listened and heard a complete thought—when I was eight. So I grew up thinking that I was abnormally normal.

I began to officially embark on a spiritual path during the time when I was carrying my third child. I asked my spiritual teacher what could I do if I was embarking on this path for protection. I just felt like protection was the main thing. I was always scared, and I just wanted to be protected so that nobody could harm me. When I asked her, she said, "Ijoma, you are your greatest protection. Everyone has everything that they need inside of them. All you have to do is to live and know that you are protected." Well, of course, I didn't know what she meant, 'cause any time I tuned in, as far as I was concerned, I was scared.

I have journeyed through many places and spaces, but I think that my most profound lesson came right before the meaning of my teacher's words really sunk in, when I was at the monastery.

Oh, you've got to walk that lonesome valley.

—Anon, "The Lonesome Valley"

I was introduced to the monastery through Jazé, my second husband. The first time that I went to the monastery I told him, "Jazé, this is not for me. I do want to develop discipline, but I don't want to stay in no monastery like this." But he was intent on going, and he proceeded to wear down my confidence and self-esteem. I just felt like I had something to prove, and my self-esteem was so low at that point that I was a prime candidate for whatever he wanted to do. So I went.

The monastery was a house out in the suburbs. It wasn't like a real, real spiritual retreat, but they did the best they could with what they had. Zenza was the spiritual leader. The women did all of the work and prostrated themselves before Zenza. All of that was supposed to deal with humility. Regarding Zenza as a holy man showed that you could recognize the divinity in everyone. When I first got there, even though they didn't tell me that I had to, I did everything. I wanted to fit in. It was really nice at first. But then of course, as with all spiritual despots, the truth began to show itself.

We would get up at sunrise, wash up, clean up, and make up our mats. We would get dressed and work, and we wouldn't eat food until after noon, based on the premise that our bodies were not able to digest food until after noon. While we were working, we couldn't eat or drink. We did have contact with others in the sense that we would go in the market and do vending, but we weren't allowed to talk to anybody other than to make sales.

We had to ask permission for everything. We had to ask permission to turn on the light. We had to ask permission to go to the bathroom. We had to ask permission to breathe. During that time, I had my three older sons from my first marriage with me, and I was nursing the baby son that I had with Jazé. My children hated it. I had taken them out of school, and it was really torturous for them because there was an elementary school right across the street from the room where they stayed. Every day they saw the kids across the street, and they wanted to be in school. They would always say, "Ma, let's leave. Ma, let's leave!" Somewhere in the back of my distorted perspective at that point, I was thinking that being in the monastery would really help my children to develop into spiritual beings. My oldest son ran away from there eventually.

I guess I didn't leave then because, again, I was feeling the need to be protected. I suppose that I was just emotionally battered, and not only that, we didn't have any other place to stay. So I adapted because I was serious about my spiritual devotion, and I thought it good to take on a monastic lifestyle. Drawing from the Christian perspective, the Islamic perspective, and certain other African religions, the monastic lifestyles fostered humility. I wanted to go through the initiations, so I just dealt with being there as a form of submission. That is how I was able to deal with it.

I began to really want to leave, but I was afraid. They took all of our money. We weren't able to talk to anybody. The phone was guarded. Everything was guarded. You were never alone. But I knew that I had to leave when my baby son was beaten. He was beaten till he was bleeding, and he was only a few months old.

See, Zenza would beat his wives, and they would always say stuff like "Well, whatever happens to you is karmic anyway." When I came to the monastery, their children were beaten too. I remember one little boy in particular who used to always have bruises all over his body. I came in there one time, and he was bound and gagged. He was only five.

Zenza wanted me to participate in these sex rituals with them. He was trying to involve me in these situations. I didn't want to participate in them, and my baby would always start crying, and that would help me to get out of the situation. Zenza was saying that my baby was crying too much.

One day while I was cleaning, Zenza told me to leave my baby son with one of his wives. He said that she would make him stop crying. But my baby was just a-crying and crying, crying and crying. So I said, "I want to go see about him." But Zenza would not let me go see him. He said, "Your son is all right." But my son kept crying. Finally, Zenza said, "I think you need to go see about your baby." I went in, and my baby's butt was raw, bleeding raw. Zenza's wife had beaten my baby until there was no skin left on him.

I was numb at that point, so I just snatched my baby up and started crying. I didn't know what to do. So I just prayed. I was really afraid. I didn't leave at that point because I didn't know where to go. I didn't know anybody in that city or anything. I didn't know what was going on or what was going to happen. So I stayed. But all the while, I was just trying my best to figure out how I was going to get the heck out of there. I was trying to figure out how I could get around where some money was so that I could get my sons. It wasn't like it was just me.

Hush, oh hush. Oh my Lord, what shall I do?

—Anon, "Oh My Lord, What Shall I Do?"

So we were abused psychologically first and then physically. The physical boundaries were overcome. It was the psychological that was a battle. After my baby had been beaten, I was silenced. I couldn't talk to anybody. And Zenza was like, "Talk to me. Just talk to me, my little lotus flower." He would say those kind of things trying to get me to talk.

I began to see, Spirit showed me, that Zenza was beginning to panic because he didn't know whether or not he was getting to me. And all of a sudden, I remembered my spiritual teacher and her saying to me, "Ijoma, you are your own best protection." The spirit told me what to do. Spirit showed me that my talking to Zenza gave him power, and it was my silence that would break Zenza's hold over me. Zenza didn't know what was going on. All the while, I was silent and constantly praying for Spirit to show me how to get out of there.

Slavery's chain done broke at last.

—Anon, "Slavery's Chain"

The next week, my first husband showed up at the monastery. He said that he came to a religious conference that was being held in the city, but I believe that he was the answer to all of our prayers. My oldest son later told me what happened.

My oldest son had gone to take out the trash when he saw his father driving along the sidewalk. He then called his father over and ran over and got into the car. As they drove around, they were talking, and my son was telling his father that the monastery was crazy and he had to get out of there. So his father said, "You can't just leave like that. You know your mother would be worried about you." And my son said, "But I can't stay either." So his father gave him two hundred dollars and told him to go on back and talk to me and let us know that we could leave. Then his father left.

His father dropped him off, but my oldest son went and snuck and hid until his father had gone. He took the money and he left. He told me later on that he felt like if he had come back, Zenza would have taken the money from him, and he felt like he didn't know whether he could trust me or not. So my son rode the bus to D.C. to see my father. When he got there and told my father what was going on, my father called and threatened to bring the FBI to the monastery if we didn't turn over my two oldest sons. He said that he didn't care what happened to me or my baby.

Zenza wanted all of us to leave at that point, when my father had called.

I remember it clearly. Zenza was screaming and saying, "I can't deal with the FBI! I can't deal with the FBI! So what do you want from me?" I said, "Give us five thousand dollars to get out of Dodge." And he did. Zenza gave us five thousand dollars, and we got on a bus and went to L.A. That was the last that I ever saw of Zenza or the monastery.

Sometimes I feel like a moaning dove.

—Anon, "Sometimes I Feel"

I don't know what was hardest, the months that we were in the monastery or the months right after we left. Jazé was so mean after we left the monastery. He was so mean. I felt like I could take up for my other two oldest sons, but they were like, man we need to get out of here. So they left. They ran away. I felt like I had a hole in my soul. I had lost my children, my life. I had lost my mind, my self-esteem. I lost my children.

It wasn't until my all of my three older sons left that Jaze started in with the physical abuse. Jazé would lock me in the bathroom and taunt me. He wouldn't let me out. Jazé would be all in my face taunting me—backing me into a corner. Sometimes I would strike out 'cause I was thinking that he was getting ready to hit me. If I struck out at him, then he would really hit me. I would fight him back, but I felt like it was just going to get worse and worse.

I remember one time, I was sitting on the porch with a huge black eye, in a daze. I was just contemplating, "What is happening? How did I get in this situation? What is happening here?" Then our friend, Sister Jasmine, came by and said, "Ijoma, what happened to your face?" I was like, "Oh, I walked into that pole over there." She looked at me like, I know that you don't think that I believe that. But she didn't say anything, and she just kept on looking at me as if she were looking through me. I said, "I was just talking to so and so, and I turned around and just, BAMM, the pole was there." She just looked at me and patted me on the back and said, "You know, you have a lot of talent. You could be doing something else with it." And then she left.

Sister Jasmine asked me to call her, but I never called her. I was too embarrassed and didn't know how I had gotten in this situation. I had never ever seen myself in that situation. I would always talk about women and say, "I don't see how they could let themselves get in that situation. I would never let myself get in that situation." I would always have something to say for other people because I never, ever thought that I would end up abused.

Easter Sunday 1992, I will never forget it. I remember seeing black and coming from this place where I was hearing all of these gargling sounds. Jazé was choking me. He was standing over me and cussing and carrying on. My baby was standing over in the corner crying his head off, and all I could think of was getting out of there. So I did. I grabbed my baby and ran down the street, knowing that Jazé was chasing me. Then Jaze grabbed me and started choking me on our front lawn. It was all of these people out there on the street who had come to the church next door for Easter service. It was just like the wildest thing. But the neighbor came up and pulled Jazé off of me, and I ran in the house and got my money so that I could just leave. I left at that point.

> *Oh my Good Lord. Show me the way.*
>
> —Anon, "Oh My Good Lord, Show Me the Way"

Some friends of mine in D.C. sent for me, so I went. I spent about a month and a half out there. When I was out there, I surprised my mother. She was really glad to see me, but she was dealing with my brother, who was on crack at the time. I have three brothers, all of whom have been on crack. One just died from a heroin overdose. Another is in the penitentiary now, for the third time. So, my mother really couldn't give me much attention. My father wouldn't even talk to me. My sons were still upset and tripping because I had not told them all of what had gone on. So they didn't really want to speak to me much.

That's why I called Jazé, because I felt like I didn't have a family. I called him from D.C. Jazé said that he was sorry. He was very apologetic and told me that it would never happen again. But he was lying. People were like, "Why are you going? Don't you know that he is the same man that you left?" In my mind, I felt like I was going back because I had to see if he was sincere. I wanted to give him a chance to prove himself. Oh, I lost a lot of friends behind that. A lot of people in D.C. were so disgusted with me.

The trumpet sounds within my soul. I ain't got long to stay here.

—Anon, "Steal Away"

So it wasn't a month—not a good month before Jazé started up again. He didn't hit me, but he was trying to intimidate me, gangster me, bully me, shove me with his shoulders about things that I didn't even do. And I was just afraid. I was a scary kind of person. It was a trip, because other times I would be so brazen, but it seemed like with certain things I was really afraid. Jazé was up to the same old stuff. Locking me in the bedroom and not letting me out. Finally I started waking up at nights. I'd wake up at about three in the morning, and I couldn't get back to sleep. Nothing in particular would be coming to me other than I felt like I had to leave.

Jazé was getting progressively crazier. He was mad all of the time. He was mad because I went to go get AFDC [Aid to Families with Dependent Children] because I was tired of not knowing whether or not we were going to have food. He'd get mad if I drank up all of the water, and you know if you are pregnant you have to drink a lot of water. He got mad because I took a little bit of money and bought a game to send to my sons. So anyway, I started having visions of doing him bodily harm—of killing him.

After one argument, I saw myself beating him in the head with my big walking stick—splitting his head open. Now I know that was my second-generation grandmother who was coming to me—talking to me. She was a slave in Texas. When the slaves were given their freedom on June 'teenth, she packed up her bags and she packed her children to get ready to leave. Her children were half-white because they were the slave master's children. Apparently, the slave master claimed that he loved her. She, of course, did not love him. When it was time to go, she was like, "Well, I am out of here." The slave master told her that she wasn't going anywhere! She would have to stay! She told him, "Not over my dead body!" He wound up beating my grandmother in the head with a two by four. He killed her that way. He felt so guilty about it that he left half of the plantation to her children.

I went there when I was a child. Beautiful land. We don't own most of it anymore. So I knew that that was my second-generation grandmother coming to me, just showing me that by any means necessary I had to get my freedom.

The next time, two days after that, I was cutting a cantaloupe. Jazé had said something, and I saw his head being the cantaloupe and me just splitting it in half with this knife. Well, I knew that that was my great-grandaunt coming to me at that point. This was all on the same side, on my mamma's side.

She was locked into an insane asylum because they said that she split her father's head open with an ax when he was asleep. All because, supposedly, he wouldn't allow her to go to the prom. I knew that he must have been incesting her, 'cause you don't just kill somebody over not going to the prom, right? You just don't do that. At any rate, they locked her up. So I felt that that was her saying, "Ijoma. Freedom. By any means necessary!"

At that point, I knew that if Jazé said anything else to me then I was going to kill him. Period. I wasn't gonna die, and I didn't want to be locked up and not be with my children, so I knew that I had to go.

I called a friend of mine and planned a getaway. Everything was working like clockwork. She came over when we knew that he was gone and was gonna be gone for a long time. When I left, that house was bare. Most of the stuff in there was mine. When I left, that house was bare.

Oh run, my loving sister. True believer got a home at last.

—Anon, "I'm Hunting for a City"

So that was the onset to my journey in healing. When I finally got into a place where I was semisituated, I had to ask myself, "Ijoma, how did you get into this situation? What went wrong? What happened?" I took a look at all of my relationships and saw how they had progressively gotten to that. I had never been in an abusive relationship before, but my first marriage had begun to deteriorate into verbal abuse, which was why I divorced him, 'cause he had talked ugly. So I had to backtrack. I had to go back to my first primary relationship with a man, which was my father. I had to go back to what happened from the womb. Going through all of that, I had to see that it began there.

My father was in love with two women. My mother went on and got pregnant, so they went on and got married. On account of all of the feelings that she had—fear and anxiety—and the feelings that he had—resentment, frustration, anger, and denial—the memories that I have as a child were always feelings of me needing to win his approval. Always.

He didn't spend a lot of time interacting with us. He worked a lot, and he ran around a lot. So we really didn't know him very well. All of us had issues with him. Growing up and becoming adults, we had to deal with it. I just remember my first encounters with him were always violent. I remember one day we had gone to the fair, and we were waiting for these people who were late. I turned around to read the pictures on the wall. I was no farther than four feet from my father, and when I turned back around, he was gone.

So I am still in the lobby area, and I am looking around and worried because I don't see him anymore. As I am walking back to the spot where I was, here he comes, coming in from the outside, fussing at me saying, "Where have you been!" I said, " I have been right here." And he said, "No you have not; you are a liar. You are lying!" I said, "Daddy, I was right here reading." Then he says, "Stop lying to me." BAMM! He slaps me across the room.

I was really devastated. We just never had a really good relationship. Those kind of situations were always coming up. It just set up a bad situation, a situation that was already unbalanced from birth. Consequently, I was always trying to please him. I began to realize that the men that I was attracted to were just like him in certain ways, and I always felt the need to have their approval. I was always attracted to people who were generally disagreeable, liked to argue, and were very controlling. So consequently I attracted those kinds of relationships in my life, and it escalated with Jazé.

The journey to healing was long and hard, but I began to realize that I was not going to be able to have a healthy relationship with any man unless first, I got in touch with the masculine energy in myself—heal that—and then approach my father and heal that relationship. So I had to begin to address the warrior in me. I had to begin to address the aggression in me, which I am still addressing to this day. I did that through meditation. Spirit gave me a particular meditation that I teach today in workshops to heal damaged lives.

At any rate, it has been a serious journey, and it always involves me looking at the fact that even when my second husband was quite violent I had to assume at least 50 percent of the responsibility for the abuse in that relationship. He could have only done what I allowed him to do. I had to check myself in many ways and come to the place where before I could point my finger to somebody else I'd have to point three of them back at me. I'd have to say to myself, "What is my lesson in this situation? What did I do to draw this energy to me? How can I deal with this for the higher good?"

Not always did I keep those things in mind, but at some point I eventually came to that.

Peace. Be still.

—Anon, "Peace Be Still"

My father and I have healed a lot. Not so much because he was trying to understand me, because he was not. But I made an effort to try to understand him, and that was what began to break him.

In truth, you cannot change other people, but we can change ourselves. So I had to understand him and where he was coming from. My father showed his love for us by providing material things. That is what love meant to him, and in his way, he felt like he was doing a very good job. But everybody wanted a hug. Everybody wanted his time. I realized that I had to change what I was looking for in a man and that I could not expect anything of anyone that I could not expect in myself. I used to have this saying that "I didn't want a man that was going to be too nice to me," because I felt like I could run over him. But I had to check myself. I was like, "What am I saying here! Why can't I have somebody who is nice to me?"

I had to really assess it all for myself, and really, it wasn't until I had just totally accepted the fact that maybe I wasn't going to get married again and maybe I'd be by myself before this man came and was really a blessing. I now have a very loving mate. Even though he looks like my father's tribe, and he has a sense of humor like my father, there are other things that are totally, totally, TOTALLY different. He does not feel the need to compete with me. He does not feel the need to control me. He don't argue with me, and I am like "Wow. This is different. I can grow to like this." I have my moments where I want to go into fire mode, but he doesn't go there with me. We do talk about stuff, but he will not argue with me. I think that arguing is still a part of my programming that I am working through and unlearning. I am still learning to be peaceful. This time I feel like there is really a strong possibility for things to evolve in a wonderful way.

My big sons and I have done our healing. We have good relationships now. I am very thankful for them. It was such a blessing. Last year, all three of them at different times, totally unprompted, came to me and said, " Ma, thank you so much for the things that you taught us. At the time we did not understand. It didn't make sense. Now we see what you are talking about. Now we see it." I just cried each time. I just give thanks, you know?

I am learning to forgive. You have to. I am finding that I still have a lot of anger about some things, so I am having to deal with that, which is good. I find that a lot of our people, because of the pain that our people have experienced, tend to lash out and want everybody else to feel their pain. I know that that was Jazé's problem. He had experienced so much pain in his lifetime. He witnessed his mother cut up one of her husbands, just all kind of stuff. It wasn't until I went to his house, met her, and saw where she was coming from that I really understood.

We do attract people and circumstances into our lives to learn certain lessons. The lesson of learning that our greatest protection is within was a very costly lesson for me. Very costly. In all of the scriptures, whether it is worded differently or not, they all say "Be still and know that I am God. Know that I dwell within you." You have to be quiet. You have to come to a place of inner peace where you can tap into that infinite source. So by coming through all of that and realizing the gifts that I had been blessed with, I asked the creator, "What can I do with these gifts to help others? What can I do to help?" I don't want anybody to have to suffer what I have been through. And Spirit was like, "You can teach."

I started giving a series of applied spirituality workshops to teach people. Basically, I help them to remember what they already know. I help them to tap into what is in them already—a world of psychic protection. I teach the basics of the spiritual path so that people can stop looking outside of themselves and thinking that they have got to set somebody up on a pedestal, because everyone else in the world has the answers but them. In this day and time, there is no excuse to ignore our direct connection with the creator. Spirit is speaking to us loud and clear. We just choose not to listen. I got tired of getting my butt kicked by the universe, literally. So I decided to start listening and doing as much as I can, in the way that I can to follow divine guidance.

Spirit is patient and kind. I got to the point where I said, "Look, I want to do it, but you have got to make these lessons easier, because they are wearing me out!" And then they started coming easier. See, we forget that, "Ask and you shall receive."

We think that we can't ask something that plain and simple. We think that it has got to be hard. Without pain, there cannot be any gain. I believe that there can be gain without pain, but we choose pain because pain is a great teacher. Pain will make you pay attention. But everything, every thought, every situation is a teacher, because it is an entity in and of itself.

Essentially, the healing has to start when you recognize the gifts that the creator has already given you, recognizing that so many of the things that we do are already ways in which we protect ourselves. All we have to learn to do is balance our energy. Spirituality is supposed to be practical—applicable to our daily living. It doesn't have to be this mystical, magical thing. Even though it can be all of that, it doesn't have to be that for you to be about it. Spirituality is supposed to be something that is tangible, something that is real. As long as it is presented as something that is way out there, then very few people will get it. The powers that be, no matter who they are, love that. As long as they can get you doing something other than making contact with the creator within, you will always be a slave of some sort or other, always under the whim of someone else, because they will determine your destiny.

I am going to sing. Going to sing all along the way.

—Anon

I am really excited about life and a lot more loving with myself. I am learning how to honor my body. I am being more diligent about dancing and doing things that bring me joy. Dancing is like church to me, making a joyful noise, leaping into the air, and giving thanks to the most high. For a long time, I sacrificed all of my time and energy to fulfill everybody else's needs that I really didn't do what I needed to do for myself. I feel that my life has been really good thus far. I just feel like my life has a greater sense of purpose, in order to help others.

Ijoma's eyes, now misty, stared out the window. As we sat in the bright room, wordless, I saw in her a little girl with a woman's gift, who could not find the comfort and the protection that she, for a lifetime, sought until she looked to God. I didn't speak to anyone that night. My mother called and so did Roxanne.

After leaving Ijoma's house, I had no words. It was as if I, too, had seen the flesh-removing blows and, like Ijoma, was silenced.

That night, I heard Kenny B's voice along with Ijoma's, and they were both saying "Have no fear." "You can't change anyone." "Everyone is in your life for a reason."

"You must forgive." "God is with you." And I couldn't speak because I, too, had fear. I, too, had anger and harsh words and wishes that others would alter.

That night, I lay in the fetal position in bed, rocking myself to sleep. The first sounds that I made after Ijoma's good-bye were moans. They were wails to God from my own wounds. They were cries for a forgiving and accepting heart—utterings for understanding.

Sleep was slow to approach, and as my head rested on the tear-dampened pillow, my heart awaited the morning sun. I thanked God that night for Ijoma. I thanked him for this—our second meeting. I told him that I was ready to take those steps toward my healing, and that night I prayed for a safe journey.

a.a., *Diva*, 2001. Acrylic on canvas, 16 x 20 in.

h sit down, sister, sit down!
I know you're tired
'Cause you come a long way;
Sit down chile,
Sit down an' res' a lit'l while.

Oh, you come a long way,
An' you had hard trials,
An' I know you're tired,
Sit down, chile!
Sit down an' res' a lit'l while!

Tell me what you're waitin' for.
I'm waitin' for my mother,
'Cause I want to tell her howdy.
Sit down, chile!
Sit down an' res' a lit'l while.

Oh, you come a long way,
An' the road's been dark,
An' I know you're tired.
Sit down, chile!

Sit down an' res' a lit'l while;
Oh, sit down, sister, sit down!
I know you're tired, sit down!

'Cause you've come a long way,
An' you had hard trials,
I know you're tired,
Sit down, chile!
Sit down an' res' a lit'l while.

—Anon, "You're Tired, Chile"

DIVA

I suppose we each had a favorite—we neighborhood kids who used to rotate babysitters. There was Maxine, who was chubby; Netta, who was skinny and fun; and Caroline, who mamma said was fast. But my favorite was Diva. Diva was from Chicago, and during the summers she stayed with our neighbor, her Aunt Pearl. Diva was smart and stern and could run faster and play harder than any of the boys I knew. Diva was determined, and it was that determination that took her from a single-parent home with thirteen brothers and sisters to graduating summa cum laude with a triple science major at Spelman, one of the most prestigious schools in our area. I admired her. People would say that we looked alike, and I remember having some pride about that because Diva had a prettiness about her; she had a strong sense of self, and I knew that whatever she did Diva would be a success.

The day that I got the call about Diva was not a good one. It was my senior year at Spelman, and I, immobilized with grief over the loss of the man that I loved, was like a zombie then. He had died suddenly some weeks earlier. The caller said that Diva had a nervous breakdown, and I pretended that it was not true. I never went to see her "in there." I used the excuse that I didn't want to see her "like that." But that was a lie. The truth was that I was scared. I was scared that in Diva's face, in her eyes, I would see something that reminded me of my own.

Diva and I hadn't spoken since before the breakdown. Three years had passed since that harrowing call, yet I continued to think of her. Afraid of mirrors and ashamed about my inaction, I'd made an art of avoiding Diva. But this evening was different.

The candle burned uneasily in my darkened living room, but this time my fears were overridden by thoughts of my prayer and promise to step fully into my own journey. The words that I had spoken after hearing Ijoma's song echoed in my soul, and this time, I knew that I could avoid neither mirrors nor the wise ones who held them. Illuminated by the candle's uncertain flame, my fingers uncurled to touch the dial, and for the first time in three years, I asked to speak to Diva.

I thought about the time that this episode took place. I thought about what was going on with me and where I had been that made this circumstance. I have come to call it mental anguish, even though some people call it a mental breakdown. Some people call it depression. But I was mad. I was upset. At the point in my life that this took place, many people would say, "How could she be so upset? She is married. She's got a house. She's got a car. She works for a Fortune 500 company. She's got it going on! Ms. Diva has got it going on! How could she be upset?

"She goes to church. She has got her son. She has got her husband and she is making whatever society thinks is a good amount of money. How could she be mad?"

Based on society's figures, I was at the top of the echelon. I had already been valedictorian of my high school, had already graduated with my triple major. For me, it was just success after success. I should have stopped. But I just kept going and going. 'Cause, you know, I kept telling myself, "I got it going on. I got it going on all the way around. I am all of that!"

I should have stopped.

I expected more than what America could give me. I expected equality. I expected that. Because, to me the civil rights movement should have moved things. I did not know that there was so much division still in the United States. I did not know that if I qualified for a position that they could still discriminate against me. I didn't know that.

Before I knew it, I had hit the glass ceiling. With my upward mobility, I was pressing myself against the glass ceiling. What was different for me in my experience, which made it so difficult for me, was that I had heard the stories of white discrimination against blacks—if I could term it that—but I didn't know that I would be discriminated against by people who looked like me.

I left my home of Chicago to work in Ohio. When I was in Ohio, I was rolling. Anything that I wanted, if I performed, I got it. So I got promotions. I could just show you the certificates and awards. I got certificates, promotions, awards, and all kinds of stuff in less than two years. I was on the fast track. Then mom got fatally ill.

My mother and I were best buddies. We were friends. She was one of my best friends in the entire world. There was nobody that I'd rather talk to than my mamma. We would talk about everything: boys, girls, dreams. . . . I was the eighth of fourteen children. She loved each one of us differently, according to his or her need. She just had so much love to give.

When I was one year old, she and my father separated because of his wild life—drinking, women, and whatever. She loved him enough not to divorce him, but she just could not have us be affected by his behavior. As long as I could remember, she was my foundation. Anything that went on, she could just about tell it by reading my face. Now she needed me.

When I got the call, it was a Friday. I was coming into the house after just having been out partying. They told me that if I wasn't back in Chicago on Saturday then I wouldn't see my mamma alive. So I locked up my house, left my car, got on a plane, and went straight to the hospital.

When I got to the hospital in Chicago, I hadn't slept. You know what the first thing she said to me was? Just like any mom, my mamma looked up from the bed and she said, "Girl, you ain't combed your hair. The bathroom is down there to the left." All I could say was, "Mamma, they told me that I was not going to see you alive."

So that is when I transferred my job and moved back to Chicago. I moved back with mamma—to take care of her. She was dying of cancer. I was twenty-four.

When you lose your mother, you lose your onliest friend.

                        —Anon, "Going to Toll in Jesus' Arms"

The time from when I first came home until the time of her death was a beautiful time. It was a beautiful time. We did everything that mamma wanted to do. It was like a life dream. We visited people every other day. We went to different church functions. We did a lot of things. We just enjoyed each other; we just enjoyed life. This lasted for about nine months.

I remember the night mamma died; we were over on Winchester Avenue in her room. She had been comatose all day. Just sleeping. Mamma was not in any pain at this time. She had been on very strong medication to stop the pain of the cancer. I did not know how badly she had suffered. I didn't know that until the very end. That particular day, mamma was sleeping, and she just woke up all of a sudden, looked up, and said, "They're coming." I was like, " Who's coming? Is somebody coming over to visit?" As I digest that now, I know that she knew that the angels were coming to get her that day.

That day, a family friend called, and he could tell in my voice that there was something wrong. He asked, "Are you all right?" I said, "Yeah." He said, "Do you want me to call the family?" And I said, "Yeah."

They called everybody in. Everybody from New York to Miami, everybody came. All of the fourteen children and their spouses came. We were all in that room. What we normally do when there is a situation that is out of our control is pray about it. We get together in our circle. When we have family gatherings, we always get in our hand-holding circle. I guess it is a symbol. I don't know where it started. But we got together, and we held hands around mamma's bed, and we sang praises that night.

Mamma did not pass until all of the children were in that room. My youngest sister had come from Miami. My brother came from New York. Everybody came. And when we were all there, without even opening her eyes, she knew. Then she looked up toward the right-hand corner of the room, and her spirit left.

It was an interesting thing because we held hands and sang through this whole ceremony, but when she left, everybody walked away and tried to deal with it in their own way. But you know what? I don't think we dealt with that adequately. As a black family, we had been trained not to express things.

I don't think that we expressed ourselves about what we felt at that time. I know I didn't because right after mamma left, I developed strep throat and couldn't talk. I couldn't talk until the funeral.

I was chosen to speak at the funeral because I had stayed with her. On the day of my mamma's burial, when I got up to the mike, the first words that I said were, "Can you hear me? It is not that this is a grieving voice."

Denial, right there. "This is not a grieving voice. . . ." I can say now that when she went on to be with the Lord, I can't say that I lost her, but when God took her, it was a big hole there. It was a big void.

Motherless child have a hard time when mother's gone.

—Anon, "Motherless Child Have a Hard Time"

I was very disappointed with my job in Chicago. When I came to Chicago, I was on the fast track. I was programming computer software. I was excellent at what I did, and they knew it. The way I understood the track was that once you had done your duties in the dungeon, you get promoted to team leader, then you get promoted to project manager, then you get promoted to management, which is what I said I wanted to do when I joined the company. Not only did I want to get promoted to management, I wanted to be an executive manager. I wanted to run some of the business. This is what I wanted to do. But that's not what happened. It became a long process of what I call capping. Capping is them saying, "You are not going to go any farther than we will allow you to."

When you get labeled, like I did, in that environment, it is hell on earth. I thought that if you do good then everything will come out right. No, not necessarily. You can do good and do well and get blackballed. You can.

This is how I had gotten rewarded for the exceptional work that I had done. The people that I had taught—who came in two years after me—were promoted to management, where I wanted to go. They were promoted to management.

They were no more qualified than I was. It is just that I was labeled. I had an extroverted personality in an introverted company. They used whatever excuse they could find. "She's too loud." "She's too emotional." "She wears. . . ." Whatever the reason was, I was not going anywhere. So this was new to me. This was new to me—that I could go and perform and be the best on the team technically, and yet, because of someone's opinion of me, I could be stifled. This was new to me.

Now this is when it became ugly. It was already bad. In my heart, I knew that it wasn't going to change, but I prayed and hoped that things would change when the next new manager came in. I always had hope that things would change. That the good would prevail. That this evil, unfair organization that was based on buddy systems would diminish. I just knew that in the 1990s this could not be going on. My company was at the forefront of the movement. "We had our laws before there was a law. We were fair before there was fairness." But I was blackballed.

I refused to give up because I wasn't a quitter. But I started distracting myself with social events. I started going out on dates more and not being available for overtime. I met my husband at work in 1990, and we were married in 1991. So in 1991 it was on!

In 1991, my company began going through a major reorganization. They were losing so much money worldwide from this good ol' boy's system that in a couple of months they went from 600,000 to 300,000 employees. They had to get rid of them. So in 1991, what I was getting was, "We know that you are a good performer, but we are just going through so much that we can't afford to promote you now. We can't afford to give you more money now. We are just hanging on, and if you just hang in there with us then when all of this passes it will be better."

I said, "Okay, I understand."

So I took maternity leave. I took maternity leave. In fact I remember telling my project manager that I was going to get pregnant because I was sick of this, and at least as a woman, I had one way out. Not that I was just going to get pregnant to leave, but since I needed to go on and have a child this was a good way to compromise. I told them, "Y'all go on and get your thing together, and I am going to go on with my life, and when I come back hopefully you'd have got things together."

So I went on leave. I planned to stay out for twelve months, but after six months I got a call from one of my brother managers. He said "Diva, you know that team lead position that you have been waiting on? I have got one for you! And you will be working for Kyle, another brother."

I got all excited.

"But," he said, " I need you to come back sooner than what you are talking about." I told him okay. I preempted my maternity plans, went back into that organization, and you know what, when they transferred me over to Kyle's department Kyle acted like he didn't know what I was talking about. They wanted me to program. Again. No team lead. No project management. It was all a big lie. It was a part of the game.

Not only that, let's say I came back on a Wednesday, they—THEY—there is a group of the chosen ones in the organization—most of them white men, they had been working on the network. They had gotten so good that they could get to my computer and let it cut up on me with them operating it from behind the scenes. I was so mad! I was mad! I was angry! I was angry because I felt like I had been violated too many times. They had my computer rebooting on me without me pressing any keys. I am sitting there trying to do my work, and they are controlling my system.

I said, "People are not going to believe this!" So I went and got this guy who worked with me. He saw them doing it, but they didn't care. It is a power thing. I think that they were doing this to say, "We control you. We control your system. We control your promotion. We control when you can come back from leave. We control you." I was hot!

I'm not used to being controlled, and I could not accept modern-day slavery; I don't care who was doing it. I became so angry that by that Friday I went home. My husband's cousin came to visit. She was about to get married, and she wanted me to meet her fiancé. I was telling her about what happened. I was telling her about my credentials and the things that I had already gone through and that I didn't have to take this.

By that night when they had gone to sleep, I had just gone on out my mind. Before I knew it, I had pulled my husband's cousin and her fiancé out of the bed, drug them down the steps by the neck, and kicked them out of the door.

I had just put them all in the scheme. I could not distinguish between the plot at work. I think at this point, I was not in control. I had been in control and managed all of this episode until this point alone. By this time, mom was no longer here, and I could not talk to her about what I was going through and manage the stress. When she was living, I would talk to her about some of these things, and we would manage it. It wouldn't get out of control. It had been six years since my mamma died—six years! The emotion took over.

> *I done left this world behind.*
> *I done crossed the separating line. So free.*
>
> —Anon, "I'm Runnin' On"

I could never get out as much as I needed to get out. I could never get it out. By this time, I would just talk to anybody. I would talk to complete strangers about my problem. I knew that I needed to get it out, so I kept talking, talking, talking, and I just couldn't get it out fast enough. I couldn't talk it out. I couldn't pray it out. I couldn't fast it out. I couldn't read it out. I couldn't figure it out. There was no answer to what I was going through. Nobody had ever explained this. It was not in *Ebony*. It was not at home on Winchester Avenue in Chicago. It was not at college. It was not in the church. Nobody could help me with what I was experiencing. Or could they? Or did they just not want to deal with that? It had built up so much that it just had exploded. That is what happened.

I was angry, and not only with them—if you remember, I am a churchgoer—I was mad that God had allowed them to do that. I was really mad with God. I was so mad with him that I didn't want to talk to him. I told God to "Talk to the hand!"

Oh, I am bad enough to be mad with God. I put my little hand up. Can you imagine what my hand looked like to God ? But I was hot! I was HOT! That night, actually it went on over to the next day, I remember feeling free. Like I could get up and just shout, like I was in church shouting. I ain't never shouted in church, but that night I felt like I could shout. Like I could shout, "I am free!"

It was a long period because it went from that Friday until that Saturday. Saturday is when that episode actually got into the system, when I actually had to go get help. I don't remember the series of events, but I remember calling on Farrakan though, 'cause I wanted some big help. I wanted somebody to blow somebody up. I wanted somebody to pay for what they had done to me—for what I had allowed them to do to me. I wanted somebody to pay for that. I know they could not have done it if I didn't allow it. I could have left. But, I was too afraid to leave. My company was a big name. Why would I leave? I kept rationalizing that now I was on their plantation and all I knew was their programming language, which was different from the rest of the world's. So though I was an expert at my company, I wasn't nothing outside of that world. Nothing. I would have to relearn everything. I wasn't ready to do all of that because I had worked too hard and I wanted them to give me my stuff, but they wouldn't give it to me.

So I remember calling for Farrakan. I remember feeling like I was in battle. That morning, I called somebody, thinking that it was one of my brothers who had been a military officer, and I was giving him the code to where the bomb was gonna drop. I thought that they were going to drop the bomb on my house, and I knew that me and my baby were not going to be here. I left my husband in the house. Because he couldn't help me, I made him part of the problem. Since he wasn't trying to help, I figured that he was on their side.

That night, while holding onto my baby, who was six months old at the time, I ran into the room and I locked the door. My baby was the most precious thing that I had in life. I think she is what kept me here. I was holding onto her, but I didn't want anyone else there, and my husband, with his little ol' timid self, busted down that locked door. He pushed the door down to keep me from doing something to myself or our baby. Somehow, he called my brothers, and they came to the house lickety split. He was telling them that I was trying to shoot him with my finger—POW!—and I couldn't kill him.

I remember, weeks before that, I was just slipping away. I was passing a shooting range, and the devil was saying, "Go in there and learn how to shoot." I was going to learn how to shoot, but mamma's teachings were fighting with these principles of me defending myself. She said, "Never bear arms. Don't have a weapon in your house because it is too dangerous. Something might happen." I could not get the weapon. But I had the concept of kill, though. What I have learned is that people who are suicidal may be homicidal first. If you notice, I wanted to get rid of all of them. But really I wanted to stop my pain, and I felt that they were causing it. So I wanted to shoot up everybody with my hand, 'cause that's all I had was my hand. I was gonna shoot them. Shoot them up. I was trying to kill them. The place that I started was at home because that is where I was. If I had been at work, then I probably would have been trying to shoot them with my finger. That is what happens to people; when they are up there killing the boss, they want to stop their pain. By that next morning, my husband was just watching me, as if to say, "What else is she gonna do?"

I just felt like he wasn't supporting me and that he was a part of the problem. A lot of times, he would say things at work, and I just put him on their team. I was just pissed with him. I told him, "When you go to work, don't talk about me. Don't give anybody any more ammunition."

He didn't know. He was just naive. He couldn't have known. His story is what caused him not to know. So I just had to accept that. But I didn't accept that at the time. I wanted to kill him with the rest of the people. He felt it. This was a long struggle.

They say that a lot of people who are suicidal will give away their most precious gifts. They give away things. I didn't know that I was suicidal. I knew that

I was homicidal because I was going to kill them all. That morning, I had packed up all of my baby's milk. I put it in a bag and packed it all up.

Afterwards I ran next door and I gave them my baby because I trusted them with her. I had built a relationship with the teenager there that I trusted, and I gave him my most precious gift. I gave him my baby. When I ran out of the house that morning, I had on a black dress, some long socks, and one of the sweaters that I just bought. It was a nice dress. When I ran next door, I just felt like it was going to be a long trip, so I put on some of my neighbor's pants. She is about two feet shorter than I am. I was lookin' the mess. My neighbor, who was a nurse, called 911, and the firemen came.

I remember during this whole thing, I selected who I would allow to see me based on the level of trust that I had in them. If they looked like they were a redneck, then they'd better not come to me because I would kick them in the face. That's the way I was. My circle was empty, and it had me in it.

I would let only certain people in my circle because I was tired of not being in control. This, I could control. This little piece, I could control. And so only those people that I trusted at that time, to whatever level, I let in. Otherwise, you'd better get away from me or you were going to get hurt.

They took me around the corner to the hospital. When we got there, I tried to jump over the reception desk to protect myself from the open door because I still felt like people were after me. As I was trying to hide, I scratched my leg. I remember one of those medics looking at me and saying, "Yeah, this one went over the coop."

They put me in a room, and I just felt like, "Oh God." I felt like I was going to be taken away from this evil place. That I was going to be with some people who had maybe disappeared from this evil America and that I was going to an island that only people who could free themselves of this evil could go. When they closed the door, I was on an elite airplane that was taking me there. Right then; and everyone that was around me were my servants, because I had deserved these.

To everybody who came in, I would say, "Go get me some socks. Go get me some water. Thank you very much." I was the queen—Diva—because I deserved it.

At that point, they decided to put me in the mental ward of the hospital. I didn't like those people and I didn't trust them, and my oldest brother could sense it. One ol' funky woman put me in a room, and my older sister stayed with me because I thought that I was flying again or something. I remember that lady coming in and me just feeling that she was evil, so I snatched her back out into the hallway and said, "Who are you? Who are you?"

She looked at me and she wouldn't say nothing, Nothing! Chile, before I knew it, my foot went this close within a centimeter of her face. I was going to kick her butt. My oldest brother held me back, he and my husband.

It was an emotional thing—very emotional.

So we got in touch with one of my brothers in New York who is a doctor, and he made some contacts at the mental recovery center. I remember this one point before we went there. Before we went to the recovery center, there was the circle; the same circle of family that I described earlier. They were around my bed, just like we were around mamma's bed on the night that she died. They were holding hands.

My baby brother was talking, and he was saying that someone needed to pray. Then he looked at me and said, "Diva, you pray." At the time that they were around my bed holding hands, I don't know what bed it was or how I got there. I didn't know where I was, but I remember that I looked up, and although the room was well lit, I could not see their faces. Everybody was a silhouette. I couldn't see their eyes. I couldn't see their faces. It was a very dark place that I was in. I remember him talking, and he said again, "Diva, you pray."

I started praying. I said, "Lord, I know that you are real. Save me. Save me. And even if you don't, I know that you are able."

And at that point, God forgave me, and I began to see their faces. I could see light. I could see things, but still I had a struggle before me, because now, the system had me.

I remember that we drove from the hospital to the recovery center, and when they mentioned that we were on our way to the recovery center, I started giving directions. My oldest brother was like, "You understand what we are saying?" I was like, "Yes. I do." Chile, I didn't know that it was me that they were taking to the recovery center. My oldest brother just looked at me and smiled, and he said, "Diva, you gonna be all right." When we got to the recovery center, the rest of the family met us there.

We pull together when there is an emergency. You can't talk to them from day to day, but we pull together in an emergency. I am laughing, but that is the truth.

We don't have a very open, honest, transparent relationship. We protect our-selves in our . . . we are private people. When we start talking about things that bother us, we are hushed. So it never gets out.

It had been a long ordeal, and everybody was waiting to see how it was all going to turn out, what was going to happen to that crazy Diva. Anyway, my sister said that I was so funny. She said that I was saying some off-the-wall stuff. That demon was surely doing some talking. They were laughing, and I was just as crazy as I wanted to be.

When we got there, they took us up a long hallway. We walked up this long hallway, and I was in control. I was walking up the hallway saying, "Do you see this? This is mine. All of this is mine." And they were my servants.

See, in my mind, here I was in my next palace. This too was mine, and mamma was around the corner. I was going to see her because I was in heaven. I thought, heaven must be like this. I had always been taught that there would be no more burdens in heaven. There would be no more trials, no more crying, no more of that, and so I wanted to be there. It wasn't like I thought that I was going to hell.

I was in heaven. 'Bout time, I thought. Where is my stuff? And where is my mamma? I was going around the corner to see my friend. I was looking for my mamma. Now honey, you know they gonna keep me, 'cause I was looking for my mamma. I felt like a burden had been lifted. In reality, they were just taking me to the office to do some paperwork.

When they took me to the recovery center that Saturday night, they had to put me on medication so that I wouldn't shoot up anybody in there, thinking that they were evil. They put me on medication and sent me to a room. I had a roommate, and the roommate was asleep. She was crazy too. So I quietly opened the door and went into the room. The room was dark, so I turned on the light. Chile, the minute I touched that light that woman jumped up from the bed and screamed, "Turn that damn light OFF!!!" I was like, "Dog. Take me back home."

Before I went into the room, I remember this. We were in the hallway. My brother and my husband were with me. We were facing these big metal doors, and the nurse turned to my brother and my husband and said, "You two cannot go any further. She has to take this walk alone."

So when I came through those doors, it was just me.

I must walk my lonesome valley. I got to walk it for myself.
—Anon, "I Must Walk My Lonesome Valley"

I had a series of sessions that I had to go to in order to get dismissed. I am used to this system, right? Perform—go. Perform—go home. So I went to all of the sessions. The whole process lasted for several months.

Well, while I was there it was like, finally, I was in a group that knew what I was talking about because everybody had the same thing going on. Finally, here were people who had all been angry or suicidal or whatever, and they came from different walks of life. Some of them were corporate executives; some were not. Some of them looked like they were motorcycle trash, but we became friends, because we had the same problems. Now, it wasn't a matter of black, white, a system, or whatever. We were all in the same boat. We were all trying to get better.

I remember going to these sessions, and on the walls there was a whole sheet of cartoon faces that match your emotions. I knew none of them. I wasn't taught about these emotions—ecstasy, happiness, sadness. What is that?

I had to find out what the emotions were by looking at the faces. Even if you didn't know the word, if you looked across and saw the faces, you could say, "Yeah, that's how I am feeling today." At this point I was twenty-eight years old and learning from the kindergarten level almost—things about myself that I didn't know. Things about what I was feeling inside. I knew that I was hot, but did that mean that I was ambivalent? I didn't know that I was ambivalent about it. All I knew is that I was hot. I knew that I was angry. I had to learn first what I was feeling, and then I had to learn how to make myself happy and satisfied.

I was always very codependent. When other people were happy, then I would be happy. This was playing out in my work environment. I was like, "Okay, all of the programs are written? Everybody happy? Okay, then I am happy." Instead of me saying "I am pissed off that I have been skipped over this many times. I am pissed off that this system does not work in the way that it has been described on paper. I am so disappointed that I will walk away."

This is what I should have been doing, but I didn't have that part of the puzzle. I didn't learn that. I have learned that a lot of kids who have younger siblings are codependent. They are used to taking care of a younger sibling. I should not have been responsible for anybody but myself. I even found that I have tried to control other people's behavior. So I had to learn a lot. In this whole experience, I have learned so much about how I feel.

When I was in therapy, I had to go through a lot of things. I used to see demons that no one else could see, and I would be taunted by them. I remember noting that I just felt like Legion. There was so much that was compressed that I hadn't dealt with.

Legion is a biblical character, and he used to live in a cave away from everybody else, and he just looked a mess. Like I did when I went into the hospital. He just looked a mess, and people wouldn't deal with Legion. Jesus finally commanded the demons to come out of Legion, and they came out. Legion then straightened himself up, and the people were like, "Is that that crazy man? That can't be him because he looks all right now!"

That's how it was. I had been so depressed for so long, and there were so many demons that I had allowed to inhabit me. Some people call it demons, some people call it depression; it has different terms, but basically, that is what it was. I had dwelled on things that were not uplifting. I had become accustomed to dwelling there. This was habit. This was day-to-day life now. To be negative, to be angry, to be disappointed—those negative types of emotions embodied my life. And too much of anything is not good. I had become comfortable there, and I had a long, long way to go.

I remember once I had gotten into outpatient I went to see my pastor. He told me to think of something good. Chile, I struggled for a week. Ooooh! I was strugglin'. I was like, let me see, is there something good? And I had to start doing things so that I could think of something good to replace those negative thoughts. It was indeed a struggle. When I went back to see him, I was like, "Whew, that was a lot of work!"

It helped so. He said it in such a way that was not offensive, and I accepted what he had told me. People can tell you the right thing, but if you don't accept it still ain't no good. So he told me this, and I worked on it, and I started reading books that were uplifting, inundating myself with positive experiences to replace the negative experiences that I had had for so many years.

And you know what? When I got back home, I looked back on my wedding invitation, and it had a scripture on there that signaled that I was not happy, even going into the marriage. I had written: "That I will see the goodness of the Lord in the Land of the Living." I was like, why would I even print that?

In other words, I had not really appreciated God's goodness on this side. I was hurting. I was hurting for years. It had to have been years—many, many years. You know I don't even want to mention the pain that began to grow back when I was in preschool—when I was molested. So over the years, there has been pain and pleasure. Pain and pleasure. That's life. That is the way that life is. Like my brother told me, it is like a roller coaster. You go up and down, up and down. But you have got to remember that you have got to monitor those downturns 'cause if you are down too long then you get depressed. I was down too long. I had these episodes, and then I would graduate or do something great. Oh, how wonderful. Float for about five or six months, and then something else would come up so that I couldn't stew in my sadness. But here was a time where the leaps did not exceed the valleys. That is why I was angry with the job—because they wouldn't allow me to get up. And this was one of the ways that I could get up. I could always control that. And then the control was taken away, and I couldn't get up. There was nothing that I could do, and I didn't invest a lot of time in other things that would allow me to get up. Like I said, I had to learn how to make myself happy, other than this job.

I have learned that I enjoy gardening and I like decorating. I have learned that I like to make things look nice, that I enjoy traveling and relaxing by the pool. I have learned that I like going out to eat. I like not being stressed out, and I like it when I can go to work and enjoy it. I have learned that I like making choices. I like organizing things and planning things. And I love managing things.

I like the fact that I now know that there are constraints in society and that there are still some "unsolveds." I am not fooled into thinking that things are the way that I would like for them to be or the way that the Constitution says that it should be. I am not fooled by that anymore. But I now again have hope that I can do some things that I enjoy that are satisfying, that make me happy, that make me even ecstatic sometimes. I like that. I like the fact that I can make choices and that I don't have to follow the molds of the world. I don't fit into a lot of circles.

I was always different. First of all, my mama and I had a very special rela-tionship in that I wanted to be around her even when I was grown, and she wanted to be around me. I wanted to talk to her. We were very close. Because of that closeness, at home I would catch it from some of my younger brothers and sisters, who would always be like, "Oh, Diva just thinks that she's all that!"

We would get into fights about it. You wouldn't believe it, but I used to be so quiet. The reason that I started talking was because I started getting whippings that I didn't deserve. See, when I get into something that I don't think that I deserve, then I am in trouble. So I got tired of getting my siblings' whippings, and I started telling everything. Telling everything until I got it explained well. So that helped to solve that problem. I was good at solving problems.

In elementary school, my grades differentiated me from a lot of my peers. So there I was, that girl. Just different. Not necessarily bad, just different. I got into so many fights trying to be a part of the group. I felt rejected. Even as an adult, I felt a lot of rejection because of my ideals and my beliefs, because of my ambitions. I felt rejected.

The family would not agree with me, but I feel rejection from my family because we don't have the transparent relationship that my mamma and I had. I feel like a lot of times, not that I think that I am all of that, but I feel the rejection of my choices. I chose not to have a baby out of wedlock. I chose to marry first, so I feel rejection from those who did choose oppositely. I feel rejection from having chosen to continue to go to school. I wasn't the first girl in the family, but I was the first girl to graduate from college. So I felt rejection from having chosen that route. You know not having a person's full support could be rejection. Insincere praise could be rejection. I feel rejection a lot. I feel rejection about being a homeowner. I was probably a homeowner before many of my older brothers and sisters owned homes. Even though they said the right things, I didn't feel the sincerity, and so I felt rejected.

I constantly don't fit into a lot of circles because I have not chosen what a lot of people chose to do. I really wanted, even in high school, to be a part of the group. Nobody wants to be isolated. Isolation is a very sad place to be. I don't think that people desire to be isolated. There are some people who really enjoy being by themselves, but I don't think that they just want to be there all of the time by themselves.

Mom was semi-by herself, but we were in that little circle together. The two of us.

I think I embodied a lot of my mother's pain. I helped share her pain. I was the person that she could let down her guard to, but it was two ways. We helped each other a lot. We helped each other. I always saw her helping me, but I didn't see the reverse. Now, I think that we helped each other a lot.

So now, let me bring you up to date.

By the grace of God I rise again. Glory in a my soul.

—Anon, "Nobody Knows the Trouble I Feel"

I had told them in my therapy that I did not want to go back to my company in the area that I had left. That I would go anywhere else, any position. And you know where they put me back? In the exact position that I had left. The exact area, the same people—everything.

The management told everybody what had went on with me. They should not have known. So when I went back, the people in the office had been laughing about me saying, "Oh yeah, I knew she would fly the coop one day."

One of the managers told the other manager, who he should not have shared it with because it was unethical for him to tell that manager, that I had just gotten back off of mental leave. That is what he told her. And she told me.

So I had to work in that environment. I didn't have to, but I chose to because I knew if I could get through that, there would be nothing else that could hold me back. I got in there, and I did the job better than I did before the anguish. I did it so well that they had to give me more money. They had to give me an award. I was accepted in this area now because I was under medication, which made me much quieter. And quieter to them was much more acceptable. But quiet didn't give me any energy. It was unacceptable to me.

I was doing well in the environment and I was looking for another position to go to. I was in line for another promotion and had been trained for the promotion. I had taken all of the classes that they require you to take. Had gone to school. And they gave this guy the promotion that I had been in line for. Here it goes again. Here we go again!

But thanks be to God, I didn't make that same mistake. When they promoted this guy—a white guy—over me and wanted me to train him, I sat down that day, and I wrote a very detailed note telling them why I would not train him. They were like, "You will too!" I was like, "No, I won't. I have created your processes, made you money, trained all of these little people that you told me to train. I am qualified and I will not train him." I refused.

"Umph." Management had to react, and they weren't happy to have to react to that. I was not ashamed. I felt like now I was in a different position. I was in the position of a change agent. I was saying, "You have already held me back long enough, and you would not allow me to go forward. But I will not allow you to treat me this way anymore. No." I remember going to my manager and asking him if he needed any extra work done, and he said, "You? No."

I was the oldest person on the team. The most experienced person on the team. I had the most qualifications for the position, and they promoted three people over me. They wanted me to train one of them, and I refused. And so they retaliated with "Okay, we are going to give you one month to find a new position. If you don't find a new position, then you are going to have to go back to programming." I said, "Really?"

They wanted to send me to another office. They had already gotten my papers signed up so they could move me. That Friday I could hear that teapot getting hot. "Whooo! I was hot!" But I said, "Wait a minute, I am not going back. I am not going back." Then I called my manager and told him that I wanted a separation package; that I wanted a divorce from the company. They gave me twenty-one days to think about it, asking, "Is it that bad?" I was like, "Yes, it is. I do not want to come back."

When I made that decision, I wept. I just wept. I was so happy, so relieved. I didn't know what I was going to do, but I knew that I wasn't going back in there.

I decided that day. I knew that I had made a promise to myself that I would leave before, but this time, I decided that I was more important than being associated with that company, and that my happiness was more important than whatever income they were giving me. I deserved better, and if I left it in their hands, they were not going to make the right decision, so I had to.

It was a very difficult position to be in because my husband liked the prestige of his wife working for this major corporation. That made him shine. Well, you know what, I was more important than the way I made my husband feel, and if all that he wanted was someone who worked for a corporation then he needed to go find someone else. I had sacrificed enough at this point. So I stepped out on faith, knowing that something will change.

It has not been an easy transition, because when you step out, when you make a move like that, confusion sets in. I prayed a lot during this period, and I read a lot and I got confirmation. "Yeah, this is the right time. This is the right move. Yes, you need to be out of there. 'Cause this is a life and death situation. You are not just talking about a job. If you remember, this pressure is what got you ready to kill everybody. This was not helping you."

So yes! Leaving was definitely in God's will.

Then I had to decide whether or not I was going to change careers. God seemed to come back to me with an idea of keeping children with mental anguish. I was like, "Lord, are you sure that you are talking to me?" So that is where I am now.

Life is a challenge. But what I have concluded is that if it never gets any better, I have another chance at life. And on this go-around, I will try to do things differently. I will try not to have to make other people happy. I will try not to overload myself with so many hours that I can't even go to a movie—distracting myself from happiness. I will take time to do those things that I like. I will take time to find those things that I like. I am going to look for those, and I am not going to compromise somebody else's agenda for my life.

I am not compromising as much on the basics. There are some basic things that I believe that God has designed for us. I believe that on this side of heaven we should enjoy some things; we should! We should be happy, and if there is anything that is contrary to that, then we need to get away from it. I was trying to get rid of it.

You need to distance yourself from that because life's too short, I say. Because you never know when your time is up. Have you lived? Have you used all of your talents? Have you enjoyed it? Have you helped somebody else? There are more important things in life than being a millionaire. Where are your priorities? Where is your integrity?

I get judged a lot about my choices. I get judged a lot, and you know I am learning not to let other people's judgment affect me as much. I do care what people say. I do care. I wish they wouldn't say those things. But I have accepted the fact that some people will say things, I don't care what you do. I am accepting that at age thirty-two.

I am making choices. Someone said to me, "Be a little selfish." It sounds strange because that was contrary to caring for other people, but it is in line biblically with "Love your neighbor as yourself." Don't forget yourself because you are your most prized asset. You are. And you can do so much for other people when you are all right with yourself. When you are okay with yourself.

So I am accepting who I am. Who God had designed me to be with my opinionated, big-eyed, loud mouth, full of expression, different attitude, different desire, different motivation self. You know, I am accepting that. And today, I am okay with me, and that has made all of the difference.

I was talking to this guy on this tour of Asia that I just took, and he said, "You know, you have had a beautiful life, except for the time that your mother passed."

And I told him, "Yes, I have had a beautiful life, including my mother's passing. Her passing allowed me to get even more of an experience, because if she had not passed, I would still be just connected to her. My relationship with God wouldn't be as deep because I would go to her and she would go to God for me. Or I would go to her first, and God would get the residual."

I didn't think my life was beautiful at the time, but now, looking back, it has been a beautiful time. It has been a beautiful life. Even the anguish has been beautiful.

As I left the company of this woman that I spent a lifetime knowing, I felt as if I had met someone new. There was a gentleness in her eyes, a softness in her spirit that wasn't there before. She seemed calmer and kinder and content with being who she was, where she was. It was as if her desire to become had transformed into a satisfaction to simply be. I admired her.

In listening, I realized that we indeed looked alike. Her story of identity and loss was far too familiar to my own. Yet after a lifetime of seeking approval and receiving rejection, Diva learned to accept herself.

Diva told me to love myself and to receive happiness. She told me to speak and release the pain. Diva told me to embrace life, and that evening, three years after his death, I sat down and wrote a letter to him, the one that I first loved, and for the very first time, I said good-bye.

a.a., *Detail from Family Quilt,* 2000. Mixed media on canvas, 24 x 36 in.

What can wash away my sins?
Nothing but the blood of Jesus.
What can make me whole again?
Nothing but the blood of Jesus.

Oh how precious is that flow
That makes me clean as snow.
No other name I know.
Nothing but the blood of Jesus.

—Anon,
"Nothing but the Blood of Jesus"

WILLAMINA

It was Mother's Day, and they invited me on a road trip. Gina and her mother, Ms. Mina, who wanted to see her mother on this spring day, let me and my tape recorder ride along. In between bickering and blowing her horn at the birds passing by, Ms. Mina, with her lips pursed, would turn her attention to me. "Girl, what in the hell are you doing back in Atlanta?" she finally asked. After scolding me for leaving medical school and threatening me of what she would personally do to me if I didn't go back to medical school, Ms. Mina said, with a little light in her eye, "So you're writing a book, huh?" "Yes ma'am," I told her. And I told her about Kenny and Ijoma and that I was seeking answers.

It was Gina who told me that her mother had an experience to share. But both she and I knew that for Ms. Mina, having a story and sharing a story were two very different things. So when Ms. Mina started talking, I mean really talking, I was shocked.

Healing comes in the blood.

You want me to tell you about the time I took a big ol' green bugger from my nose and put it on my brother's sandwich? Do you want me to tell you about the time I took the rake and banged holes across the top of my other brother's head with it? He says that's the reason that he is crazy now. Or do you want me to tell you about the time that I slapped my white friend? Oh, I used to do all kinds of crazy stuff. . . .

I was a real hyper child. Had I grown up in this day in time, they would have put me on some Ritalin. I was so hyped up running all over the place that I didn't even realize that I had titties until I ran outside with no shirt on and the boys pointed and said, "Oooh, look at Mina! Girl, you need to put on a shirt. You got some titties coming up on you!" I was thirteen years old then.

When my period came on, I ran up under the house and stayed up under the house all day because I didn't want anybody to know it. I heard my mamma tell my daddy, "Mina up under the house 'cause she became a lady today." Oooh, I was so mad at her that I could have beat her up for telling my daddy that.

I got a whipping every night. I did. Every night. I used to pick at my sisters and brothers. I was tired of them. I was the oldest of five, and every time you looked around, it seemed like my momma was having a baby.

My great-grandmamma used to live with us. She was Cherokee—full-blooded Cherokee Indian. Grandmamma Lena. So she would go outside all of the time and get all of these remedies out of the woods, and she would stop whatever was ailing us. Grandmamma Lena was a beautiful deep-brown woman with long straight-curly hair. She lived with us from the time that I was a baby. Grandmamma Lena was my great-grandmamma, but she raised my daddy, too. Before her husband died, he asked my daddy to take care of Grandmamma Lena, and my daddy said that he would. My daddy is a loving, blessed man. When her husband died, he took her right in.

Grandmamma Lena didn't particularly like me. We didn't particularly like each other. I was a selfish little kid, and I was tired of all of those folks in my house. Grandmamma Lena would say that she was going to pray for me all of the time. She used to compare me to my sister. She would say that I was always doing stuff that I had no business doing, and then she would look down at my toes. When I was growing up, my toes were really close together, and my sister's toes were really far apart. So Grandmamma Lena said that I was going to drop straight to hell because with my toes so close together, I couldn't fly to heaven. She of course then said that my sister was going to heaven because she was a much better person. She told me that the more I become a better person, the more my toes would get further and further apart. Anyway, as the years went on, I would watch my toes. My toes are not close anymore.

Oh then my little soul's going to shine.
—Anon, "Oh Then My Little Soul's Going to Shine"

I knew that Grandmamma Lena loved me, but I didn't care. She loved us, all of us, but I was that kind of child that would irritate you. I was just into stuff. So we weren't close. She was closer to my other brothers and sisters.

My nose used to bleed all of the time. Up until the time that I was ten years old, Grandmamma Lena was the only one that could fix it. I was a busy, overly active child, and I guess those nosebleeds was one way of my body cooling down at night. Grandmamma would get up and do something, and it would stop. My nose would bleed just about every night. I don't remember exactly what Grandmamma Lena would do, but whatever she would do, my nose would stop bleeding.

One night, my nose got to bleeding really bad. My mother and father came in and tried to stop it from bleeding. They didn't want to wake Grandmamma Lena because she had been feeling bad that day, and they felt like she needed some rest. That night was something because my nose started bleeding heavier that it ever bled before. Ever. It was just pouring blood. I remember thinking, "Oh gosh, I'm sick now."

Then mamma and daddy were like, "We're gonna to have to wake up Grandmamma 'cause she's the only one that can stop this bleeding." They went in her room and tried to wake her up, but Grandmamma would not wake up. Grandmamma Lena was going into a deep sleep. Mamma and daddy called the ambulance and a neighbor to watch us, and that ambulance took Grandmamma Lena to the hospital. Grandmamma still hadn't woken up when the ambulance came. By the time my daddy called back to say that everything was all right and that they got Grandmamma to the hospital in time, my nose stopped bleeding, and it never bled one drop again. Never.

See, it was an issue of blood with Grandmamma Lena because she had a mini-stroke. When the blood in her head started flowing again, my nose stopped bleeding. I helped my grandmother to live. They said that if we had not tried to wake Grandmamma up that night, then she would have died in that bed.

Now that I look back on it, I think me and my Grandmamma were kindred spirits. Even though we never liked each other. Maybe we were too much alike.

I was a difficult child, but that one thing I did do. That night, unbeknownst to me, I saved Grandmamma Lena's life.

I told you this story because later on in life, I realized that sometimes our pain is for someone else's healing. Sometimes we are put in difficult spaces to help some other kindred spirit along the way. I have to remember that sometimes. And when I do, I think of Grandmamma.

That's all I want to say.

The car hummed, and Gina, in the back seat, was beaming like a sunned flower. By the time my lips began to form a thank-you, Ms. Mina started honking her horn and complaining about birds and their bodily excretions. But we knew that something sacred had been shared. And on that spring day, the cool wisteria-scented air filtered in through cracked car windows; as we rode into the road ahead of us, our hearts were warm.

a.a., *love supreme,* 2000. Acrylic on canvas, 16 x 20 in.

*S*eek and ye shall find;
Knock and the door shall be opened;
Ask and it shall be given,
And the Love came trickling down.

My brother the Lord has been here,
My sister the Lord has been here,
My brother the Lord has been here,
And the Love came trickling down.

   —Anon, "Seek and Ye Shall Find"

LOVE SUPREME

I grew up hearing the words of women worn from loving too hard and too long. After my friend died, I equated love with pain, and I, the little girl who still nursed her bruise three days after the doctor's shot, vowed that I would either leave as soon as I saw love's needle of pain approach or never love at all. Being a writer, I had perfected the "Dear John" letter to an art. I composed poetry to be recited at the first chance or excuse I could find for leaving. For I would not be hurt, again. I would not be bruised, again. I had given up on love.

It was my aunt who told me about them, the two whose touch, even after sixty years of marriage, still kindled warm fire. Her name was Ms. Ruby; his, Mr. Isaiah, and when I called to introduce myself, their voices were kind.

Some days later, as I settled onto the footstool placed between their recliners, I found myself in the midst of a rare and precious treasure. I watched him, unashamed, gaze tenderly into her eyes. I watched her rest her hand on his forearm, gently. They shared a knowing smile, and calmly, with the voice of a woman wise from the width of years, Ms. Ruby began.

Sometimes I think I'm ready to drop. Trouble will bury me down.

—Anon, "Poor Me"

Me and Isaiah, we met way back in 1939 before I had my first child. I guess, like anybody else, he was just a man looking for a woman. But I was not a woman really. I was a sixteen-year-old child.

Isaiah used to slip by and pick me up. Even though he'd take me out, it wasn't like we were intimate. He was just wanting to give me a good time. Once Isaiah took me and a friend to Memphis, and when it was time to go, Isaiah and I lost each other. Night came, and me and my friend could not get back to Holly Springs. Holly Springs, Mississippi, is where I lived at. Then we came upon Jameson, a guy that I used to be interested in, but never intimate with. Jameson said that he would get us a place to sleep that night where one of his friends was. We wound up staying in Memphis for a week. It was during that time that I got pregnant with Jameson's son.

I had my first son, and Jameson left. I was never a person that would run after a person. I mean, I could hurt, really be in love and hurt, but I would never, never, show it. I tell you, after I got pregnant and Jameson left, I hurt. It was like an outcast to be pregnant and not have a husband.

After Jameson, I didn't soon have no dealings with another man. By then I was seventeen. When my son was eleven months old, one night my mamma kept him and I went down to the fair. While I was there it started raining, and as I was walking back home, Robinson, this young married man I knew, drove up behind me and yelled from his car window, "Ruby, let me take you out of the rain!" I tell you, it was raining hard that night. But I first said, "No thank you, Robinson. I am gonna run it. It wouldn't take me that long to run."

He was like, "Girl, come on. You know I am just going to give you a lift home." But when I got in his car, he didn't go the way home. He went down to where the creeks were, and he just . . . Me and him, we really fought and fought. Because I had told God and myself that I wasn't going to have any more dealings with anybody else after Jameson. I knowed what I had done to my mamma. Robinson raped me that night, and afterwards he left me by the creek.

When I went home, I didn't say anything to anybody because I actually reasoned in my mind, "Who's gonna believe you? You've got a baby; who's gonna believe you?" It was like an outcast to be pregnant and not have a husband.

So I took it, and when I went home, I took my hands and kept mashing down hard in my navel. Just a-mashing and mashing, trying to get whatever was in there out. It didn't work. I got pregnant from that very one time.

He heard my cry and pitied every groan.

—Anon, "I Love the Lord"

Anyway, I went to work again and started working, trying to take care of my babies. And guess what, Isaiah started picking me up again. Me and him weren't intimate or anything. I just needed a ride to go to Memphis to go to work. Isaiah would come to take me to South Memphis to go to work, and then he would pick me up from my job and stop me off to the grocery store so that I could buy baby food and all of this stuff with my little money. It was during that time that I ended up having a nervous breakdown.

I just don't know where my mind was, but I think that during that breakdown a lot of my hurts was lost in it. It was just more than I could deal with. It was almost like I went to sleep and I just didn't want to get up. I just didn't have no life.

When I had the nervous breakdown, I was placed in the hospital. It was a very strange thing. It was just like in this nervous breakdown, I closed the world out of me. The world didn't even exist. That is how dumb my brain seemed to be like. It just let go, and there was nothing. Everything was a dream—or nightmare—or something.

My mamma, she didn't visit.

I stayed in there, and Isaiah started visiting me in the hospital. I was there for over a month. Even though while I was in there I'm sure everybody was talking about my state, Isaiah would always tell me, "Bee, you look the same. To me, you haven't changed at all." Isaiah would come regular, and every time he would bring me things like candy or flowers or chocolates.

After I got out of the hospital, I had lost so much weight and was so small that everybody thought that I was really sick. They thought that I had caught something in the hospital and stopped coming around. But Isaiah, he came around.

That was the first time that I ever spoke up. I spoke up to Isaiah. I looked him straight in the eye, and I said, "Isaiah, I am gonna tell you something." I said, "I appreciate all that you do, but, the next time you turn that corner and you head toward our house, you'd better be coming for a wife."

You know, the way my life looked, I was the biggest nothing. But I told him that. I told him, " Don't even think about it. Don't even think about heading this way unless you're coming for a wife." And sure enough he came. Not too long after that, we were married.

At that time, it was a real statement for a man to marry a woman with children. Even though I wasn't a woman, nobody was taking that into consideration 'cause when I married Isaiah, I was nineteen years old. Still probably trying to find my way.

Crying free grace and dying love. To ring those charming bells.
> —Anon, "Mary and Martha"

After we were married, I don't know what happened, but me and Isaiah got into it, and I put him out! I put Isaiah out, but I didn't have no money or no job, so I was worrying about how me and the children were going to get food and pay the bills. Lo and behold, the weekend came, and here comes Isaiah. He gets my oldest son, who is now three, and takes him, and they go to the grocery store to buy groceries. Now, Isaiah don't know how to buy groceries, so he went and he bought all of this butter and stuff. He brought those groceries back to the house, and then he went and paid the rent for the week. After he had done all of that, he said, "Okay, now you all are okay. I'll see you." And he left. Now Isaiah did this after I had done put him out.

It was just like something that was evidently meant to be. I laugh at him all of the time because I was like, "WOW! You came back." I tell you, even if you dirty something, if there is enough prayer, then you are going to clean it up. You will clean it up.

So, after that, I let him back in.

We used to do the silliest things to keep us laughing. You would have to imagine this house that we were living in. It was a four-room house with rafters. The kitchen was cut like an *L* and the bathroom was right next to it. And the rafters in this house! Once, when I was pregnant, Isaiah wanted to see what I looked like naked. I never would let him see me naked. That day, Isaiah was determined. While I was in the bathroom, he got up and he crawled over the rafters in the kitchen so that he could get a look at me. Now I am in the bathroom taking care of my business, and I look up and see two big ol' eyes peeping out at me! So I start yelling and screaming! Now you gotta imagine, we are living in all of these little row houses. So the people in the community hear me yelling and screaming, and all of them come running. Isaiah, in the meantime, is still stuck up in those rafters. They came pouring in, saying, "What's wrong, Ruby? What's wrong?" And after I realize it is him, I said, "That ol' Isaiah is peeping over the rafters at me." Now by this time, Isaiah is stuck trying to get down from those rafters. He was so embarrassed.

We used to do the silliest things. There was a lot of laughter; there was a lot of pain, but we laughed more than the pain.

I look at my hand and my hand look new.
I look at my foot and it look so too.
Coming together in the morning.

—Anon, "Oh Lord These Bones of Mine"

Once we moved to Tupelo, Isaiah and I didn't leave each other no more. We decided that we were in this thing for the keeps. Our neighbors had been taking our children to Sunday school, by then, me and Isaiah started going to church. That was a funny Sunday. That Sunday, it looked like I had done everything; I had cooked, cleaned, and was just like, "Oh, what a morning for me and my husband to stay home and be lovers." Oh, I didn't want to go to church. I mean, when did we ever have such a quiet and sweet house?

We began to get ready for church, but that particular Sunday morning, I told Isaiah, I said, "Isaiah, let's just stay home and be lovers." And let me tell you, Isaiah has never been the type of person that will turn down lovemaking. If you ever wanted to weaken him, that was his most soft area. And you know what Isaiah said after I had done whispered in his ear? He said, "Bee, the children are expecting us. We told them that we were going to church, and that is what we are going to do." It was like I just had been slapped in the face! This man turned down this great offer! Honey, I was shocked.

So he turned me down. And that was the morning that I committed my life back to Christ. It was some change, too. He watched me for about a week or two, and he said, "Bee, I don't know what it is about you, but whatever it is, I want it because you are a changed person."

So he went about two weeks later, and he committed his life to Christ. And then our love got stronger. It just began to climb uphill. It was such an awesome change in our life. My oldest sons were teenagers then, and they saw the change. During this time, while we were living in Tupelo, nobody knew that they weren't Isaiah's children. To me that was a testimony because he was so good to those children and still is.

Before Isaiah got saved, he did drink. He would drink beer and stuff. The children changed him there, too. One day we were coming from somewhere, and Isaiah had been drinking. He got so sick that he needed to stop the car to upchuck. When he did that, the boys laughed him to scorn. They really embarrassed him. That day he said, "I promise God and me that I am never going to drink like that no more!" And he didn't.

Isaiah's promises are real. It was his promise that caused him to give up that bottle, and it was his promise to the children that brought me back to God. But I tell you, I can't till this day believe that my husband turned down such a great offer. The house was clean, the food was done, the wind was cool—and he turned me down! My goodness, my goodness, that is just still hard for me to believe.

Anchor believer, anchor. Anchor in the Lord.

—Anon, "Anchor in the Lord"

The boys saw the softness of our spirits—those soft words, those soft glances in the house. They saw the change in us. We had those times where the children would put us through so much, but it drew us together. Isaiah and I would just go into our room and pray and cry out to God together, and God would always work it out.

By then, Isaiah was working and I was driving the school bus when he ended up with the cancer. When Isaiah was in the hospital, it drew me to where I wanted to be there for him. I don't even know where the strength came from. I remember my children telling me, "Mamma, go home and go to sleep. We don't need both of you in the hospital." But they don't know that I was getting energy from God. I had to whip from the job, to Isaiah, then go back to the job, then to Isaiah. But even in his sickness, Isaiah was right there, and he was so spiritually strong. Isaiah was strong in God when he was in that hospital bed. I heard him speaking tongues like I never heard him speak before, and I knew that man was reaching out to God in a special way. We beat that cancer, me and Isaiah. With the Lord's help, we beat that cancer down!

Weep no more for baby, my heart. Weep no more for baby.

—Anon, "Weep No More for Baby"

After Isaiah recovered from the cancer, we built another house out in the country. By then we were so close together and trusting God that we could almost sense what the other one thought. I drove the school bus, and for some reason, when I would take those children home in those nice big houses I would want one for myself. I would look out over the bay, and I would say, "God, you are my God. I know that you are my God, and if you are my God, then you love me just as much as you love them. I want one of those big houses. " I just had that faith knowing that he would do it for me.

Not too long after, we built this nice big house out in the country. By then, all of our children were grown, and it was just me and Isaiah. And then my second son was killed. That was another real blow in our lives. Looking back on it, I think that was the biggest. Like Fred Sanford used to say with his hand to his chest, "That was the big one!"

You know, it almost devastated me. In the mornings when I would wake up, I would think, "This is not real. This is just another nightmare." You know, just like in that nervous breakdown that I went through. The things that a mother goes through when she loses her son is not really known to a lot of people.

I would say, "God, I know that there is something here that I need to understand." And then you go from that to saying, "God, did it hurt? Did it hurt my son?"

I actually had an experience, and after that, my heart did get damaged. I told God, I said, "I want to experience what it is like to die like my baby died." Honest to God, one morning I was laying in bed, and I felt my whole spirit just leave my body, and the spirit said, "It was just that easy. He felt no pain."

I went through so much. You know, after everybody gathered around and when all of the friends came and all of the friends left—it was just me and Isaiah. Not even our children could hardly hang around us. For twenty-one days, I could not eat. I could only sometime when my mouth would get parched, drink some water. I looked like the point of death after that. I just wasted away.

During that time, a lot of my anger was not for nobody but God. I just could not believe that he would let that happen to me. I had all of these things going on through my head, but Isaiah, he was always strong for me.

That really brought me and Isaiah even closer together. I mean it was like, "We are in it. We are in it, and we are going to go through it together." And we did.

We came through it, and we came out stronger than we had ever been. That is why I say—a lot of times—you don't like pain, but pain strengthens you to be able to deal with this life that we live in. What is funny about it is that none of us are going to go through it without the pain. Whether you are a Christian or you are a non-Christian, you are going to suffer if you live in this life. Nobody likes pain. I tell God now, I say, "Lord, I want to draw closer to you, but could you not give me no more sorrow." But in all of the pains, in all of the sorrows, it was always thick love holding me and Isaiah together.

The front wheels a-runnin' by the grace of God
and the hind wheels a-runnin' by love.

—Anon, "O Mary, O Martha"

My sister told me, she said, "Ruby, you know what marriage really is? It is two people united as one where when one hurt, the other hurt. And it is a ground that is laid out that you will get old and caring and loving together."

And I found that to be true because I was a nut. It didn't take long for me to see that the man of your life—that really loves you –he is the one that is gonna come. Yes, he is the one that will be there with you.

I told my husband once when I had surgery, I said, "Isaiah, as soon as they take me out of that operating room, you stand right there, and you make sure that my teeth is in my mouth. And check my eyes to make sure that they are not full of cold."

That is what we have done. Over our lives we have been there to make sure to check each other. To make sure that there is no cold in his eye—or his teeth is in—or you know, just to watch over each other.

I can see now the benefit of a true and a godly marriage because you are always caring for one another. You are always looking out for one another. It is always more about what makes the other person happy than what it makes you.

If I told a young person that, they might not be able to comprehend it. But that is what love really is. It is not so much you. It is what the other person wants. And it not only stops with him, it will be with anybody. "What can I do today to make somebody happy?" Because when you give others joy, God automatically brings joy into your life. He is not going to let you give and not replace that. So that has been one of the things that I have learned. It had been a lot of years, but it sure has come home to me—that it is so good to love.

It is so good to look over each other's faults and look to the better part of each person. Neither one of us, we are not educated to the point to say that, "Oh, we are all that." But I think that God has honored me and Isaiah because we were willing to do it his way, 'cause our way sure wasn't working. It was not working. It was two people making each other miserable—always.

The bills did more crushing in our life than I think anything else. It was never about women, and we went out, but women was never a problem. I don't know why; I might have been cocky, but I felt like I was more than enough woman for Isaiah.

You know, like I told somebody a long time ago, when a woman has a husband, she has to know that she has got to bring enough into it to make her feel cocky. I was telling a young girl that the other day. I never felt that I was just the refined, beautiful woman, but I thought that I brought enough to the table that I didn't never think that another woman could do what I could do. You gotta feel good about yourself.

> *I built my house upon a rock. No wind, no storm can blow it down.*
>
> —Anon, "Bound to Go"

I was preparing to retire, and we were building our dream house from our savings. I said to myself, "I really believe that if we start building this house we can finish and we won't owe nobody," and that is what we did. That house had three thousand and twenty feet in it, and it was sitting on two and a half acres. It was valued at nearly three hundred thousand dollars.

We had heard about the tornado that Sunday, and our faith in God was so strong that we just knew that God was going to take care of us and that house. We had built it ourselves, so we knew that it was built strong.

Out there in Mississippi, we get all types of storms. But I am telling you, when that storm came, it sounded like trains passing. Me and Isaiah, we prayed! I have high blood pressure, and when I get upset, my mouth gets dry. Well, my mouth got dry! I was walking around with a gallon of water and sippin' it like an old drunkard. I was a mess.

Me and Isaiah, we got down on our knees and we prayed and we prayed. But that tornado, it started busting open the windows in the house. Our next-door neighbor—he was building something and had a pile of stones in his yard. As the winds blew, those stones started coming through the windows. The enemy of his soul told my other neighbor to park his dump truck with the wire and all other kind of junk on it on the other side of my house. That truck turned over, and all of the debris went to flying through my other windows. Now mind you, me and Isaiah were in the house! And when those stones and wires started coming through the windows, I told Isaiah, I said, "Isaiah, let's go out in the Cadillac. They say that they are tight cars. If we go out there, we'll be okay." So me and Isaiah went out there and laid down in the floor of that Cadillac. Now Isaiah don't get hot. If he is sitting next to that fireplace, he is not going to ever say that he is hot. But after we were in that Cadillac for a couple of minutes, Isaiah started sweating and said, "Ruby, we have got to get out of here. I am hot!" I think he was just scared.

Anyway, we climbed out of the Cadillac and got in the closet. Now I had been praying the whole time, and by this time, I done prayed out. I don't know another prayer. I just gave up. I got under the covers, so that when the tornado smashed, it wouldn't smash my face. I didn't want my face smashed up. So I got under those covers, and the wind of the Lord just put me to sleep. I went to sleep curled up against Isaiah with my bottle of water in my hand.

When we got up and climbed out of that closet, we listened, and it was as quiet as snow falling. Evidently, the storm was over. I stepped out in our once beautiful kitchen and looked and saw that everything in the house was destroyed, everything except for the closet that we were in. When we got out into the garage, all kinds of boards and things had fallen on that Cadillac.

That is when I heard the voice. The voice that said, "I have better for you." I tell you, I never cried. I had confidence in God. If he said that he had better for me, I believed him. I shed not one tear. Me and Isaiah got in our old beat-up truck, and we drove away from that destruction.

That truck took us out of Tupelo. It was just like a tractor rolling over those trees and wires. We went back to Holly Springs, and we found out that all of our family was still alive. We know that it was God that brought us where we are, all of the way. It was God who has brought us.

So me and Isaiah we went back to Holly Springs and climbed in my brother Jacob's bed and went to sleep. Around about that time, Jacob, who was like a twin to me, had cancer. Isaiah took care of him with the same kind of tenderness that he took care of my mother with before she died of Alzheimer's. I tell you I have been blessed with a good man. I can just never thank God enough for the kind of husband that he gave me. To me it was enough that he could love the children, but that he could love my family too! When my brother was dying of cancer, he took care of him. Every day he took care of him. Isaiah has always been there for my family.

We do a lot for people. But whatever we do we never seem to get it from where we put it. God is always giving back to us in one way or another. He is just blessing us and blessing us and blessing us. It just shows that when you have love the way that God says have love, that is all that you do. You just love and let God handle his part. I had a hard time understanding that.

Isaiah was always a lover. He was always a lover. He never looked down at nobody. I'll do it now. I'll go to the old folks home and hug people and then soon after want to go and wash my hands or something. But, Isaiah, he don't never think like that. He is just a lover. A person who is like, "I love you, and God will take care of me." Isaiah has always been a person that just flows in love. I'm like, I love you, but I am going to take care of washing my hands.

And the love came trickling down.

—Anon, "Seek and Ye Shall Find"

My son kept telling me, "Mom, you have gone through so much in Tupelo. You need a change. You need to be around different people that don't remind you of all of the pain that you went through. You should come to Jackson." And he was right, because I really did enjoy moving to Jackson. Our house in Jackson and the yard is better than the one in Tupelo. Just like God said, he had better for us.

From the money that we had left over with the tornado insurance, we were able to move into this here house, and I tell you, we don't even have a house note. Once God speaks to you, you don't have to question it. You don't have to question it. All you have to do is be directed.

We came up here and we lived here. We were very comfortable thinking that we were in a very safe neighborhood and that we were just all right. By now, me and Isaiah are both in our seventies. We would walk around and just enjoy ourselves.

Any time I wake up, I would always get a cup of coffee and sit in the kitchen and read my Bible. One particular morning, I was sitting to the table reading my Bible while my son was reading a motivation book over the phone. I was listening because I always listen to my children. You know that the biggest problem with old folks is that we want to talk all of the time.

Isaiah had gone out that morning and walked, and he came back and he left the garage door open. He went in the back and laid down and went to sleep. At that time, we had a boy who was staying with us because he needed a place to stay while he was finishing school. So, like I said, I was sipping coffee and talking on the phone to my son when I saw this car pull up in the driveway. I thought that it was the boy coming back to pick up something. So I just kept talking. While I was on the phone with my son, I heard the door go "BAMM!" I didn't know what was going on. Then I heard it again, "BAMM!" and then that man busted in. I tell you the gun must have been that big! When he came in, I just dropped the phone, and let me tell you, when he put that gun to my head I was silenced. But in my heart, I was like, "God, I don't believe this!"

The thing that really grieve me is that when a black boy see a woman as old as me he would have to remember that he has a grandmother, and for him to hold a gun right to the temple of my head. . . . But something said call on the name that is above every name, and I just started chanting, "Jesus. Jesus. Jesus."

He said, "Get the money. Get the money!"

And I am just chanting, " Jesus. Jesus."

He had that gun to my temple, so I walked over and tried to look for my pocketbook. In my spirit, I was like, "If you have got to die, you will not take Isaiah with you."

He had asked me if there was anybody here, but I just kept saying, "Jesus."

By that time, who he serves caused him to start cursing me, and Isaiah heard him in the bedroom. Isaiah said that he heard the voice, but he thought that it was the children playing around, but when he heard profanity, he knew that it was not our children. So Isaiah woke up and was like, "God, where is the gun, and where is some bullets?"

And I kept saying, "Jesus. Jesus. Jesus."

My husband, when he opened the door, the door made a screeching sound and it frightened him. The man had to take the gun from my head to point at my Isaiah, and when he did, I scooted under his arm and ran into the closet. As I was scrunched down in the closet, I am still just saying, "Jesus. Jesus. Jesus." And all I am hearing is gunshots. I am hearing gunshots. He shot at my husband five times. I was in that closet. I am going to tell you, when the spirit of God is in you, it rises up and is there when you most need it. I had prayed many times to be anointed, but this time I really needed it, because by now I was almost hysterical. I was out of control and just saying, "Jesus. Jesus. Jesus."

And then my spirit said to me, "Shut up!"

Because here I am in the closet calling Jesus, and if that man had heard where I was, he would have come to get me. Spirit was like, "Shut up!"

So at that point I shut up.

My mind just that quick flashed and was like, "Your husband is going to be out there dead, right in front of you." That is just what I saw.

When I heard the ceasing of the guns, I climbed out of the closet. I didn't see Isaiah. I tell you, that was the most quiet moment of my life.

Then I heard something say, "Bee?" I said, "Isaiah?" And then I looked around, and I saw my husband standing there with his back straight and this worn-out shotgun in his hand, and I screamed, "Isaiah!" I screamed. "Isaiah!!! Isaiah!!!! Oh thank you, Jesus!"

He was alive!! He was alive!! He was alive!!! I was so excited because my Isaiah was alive. I still get so excited when I think about it. I tell you that was one day. I will never forget it. God had it fixed where he was not going to let the enemy destroy us. Isaiah meant to kill that man that day. He missed his head by an inch. After that, that man ran and busted through a window trying to get out.

My son, he bought a big old trophy for his daddy after that. He said, "You know, daddy could have jumped out of any window and save his self. It takes a special man to do what he did. Daddy walked out there to lay down his life for you." He said, "He is a proven man, because many men will say 'I will protect my wife,' but when the guns and bullets start flying, they do not stand there." That is when you know that you're loved. You're loved.

And she'll rise in his arms.

—Anon, "'Round about the Mountain"

But you know, the response of it was that time and time again. Me and my husband walked with God and with each other. Only Christ Jesus gave his life for us, and anybody else that would lay down his life to save you, to me, that is not love in speech. That is love in action. It really is. It is love in action. In all of the things that we have been through, it has always been "We are together. We are one."

There is no division nor separation. We are one. And every time that we have been through something or go through something, we get stronger. We don't leave one another. When people see us, I am sure that they be saying, "Is this for real? Are these two old folks really in love like this?" Honey, it is as real as the breath we breathe.

It is not like we don't have some times where I don't say, "Isaiah, do you plan for your maid to come and pick up your shoes?" Oh, we go through that. That is nothing, 'cause he is going to pick them up when he gets ready anyway. But the things we have been through have just been such a bond.

I'll tell you the truth. I love Isaiah. The only thing that I think I love more than Isaiah is God. And I have children, but I do know that there is a place for my children and a place for my husband, and when my children was nowhere to be found, Isaiah was there.

And it is not like you say, you love him because. . . . You love him in spite of and because of. I love him in spite of his shortcomings. 'Cause he will drop his shoes, and it will bother me. But in spite of those things, I love him. I don't look to his little faults; I look to his strength and the fact that I can say, "Let's pray," and he'll be right there praying with me and sometimes out-praying me.

Many times, I was telling my sister this, I believe that kind of love keeps healing. Not that you don't get sick, but it causes healing. I have been here, and we sit in our chairs, and I would just begin to massage his arm, and he would say, "Bee, I had so much pain in my arm, but after you touched it, the pain went away." I remember lately the arthritis in my hip was bothering me one morning as we were dressing for church, and I had to stop. I said, "Isaiah, I know that we are on our way to church, but my hip is bothering me so bad. Can we just stop and pray." And he just rested his hand on my hip and prayed for me, and that pain went away, just like that. Even in the bed, if we start massaging each other. 'Cause a lot of time when the sex is gone, honey just the touch will do . . . but as I was saying, a lot of times he will say, "I just don't feel good," and I will encourage him in the Lord and massage him, and the pain will be gone. According to his doctors, they say that they don't even know how Isaiah's back works; it is so scarred from the cancer. That was his disability, and I tell him sometime now, he is seventy-nine, I say, "Isaiah, I don't think you walked better than this when you were a young man. But I think it is because of the love."

God intends for us to be there for each other. I think that that was one of the things that clicked in later. Isaiah is kind to me because he is a man, and men are supposed to be kind to women. I just think that God gave me the best man on earth. Isaiah has been my best friend, and that friendship came during the hard times, even though I didn't understand it. Isaiah was there, and it was his healing love that brought me through many of the storms in my life. I even think back to when I had that nervous breakdown, before we were even married. Isaiah was there encouraging me.

I tell you. Love is a healer. And I just wanted to tell you about some instances where love is proven. Many times, I just thank God. I just thank him that he gave me a husband that loved me, but more than me, he gave me a husband that loved God. Isaiah loves God. And that love just keeps us going. Like that battery, it keeps us going and going and going. . . .

By then, Mr. Isaiah's back was straight, but beneath his rugged mahogany cheeks there was blushing. They again shared a smile. This indeed was her tribute. It was her testimony to Mr. Isaiah and the healing powers of God's love, and it was my reminder that doctors' needles inject substances that make us strong. It was early summer then, and the calm afternoon breeze wrapped itself around me as I walked from their home. A cardinal lifted its voice to the heavens. I shared a smile with the sun. Some months later, while rushing down a busy Atlanta street, I too met a strong and gentle man, and this time I vowed to love.

a.a., *Remedy,* 2000. Acrylic on canvas, 3 x 4 in.

Lord I keep so busy praising my Jesus
Keep so busy praising my Jesus,
Keep so busy praising my Jesus,
Ain't got time to die.

'Cause when I'm healing the sick,
When I'm healing the sick,
When I'm healing the sick,
Ain't got time to die.

'Cause it takes all of my time,
To praise my Jesus.
If I don't praise him,
The rocks gonna cry out,
Glory and honor, glory and honor,
Ain't got time to die.

—Anon, "Ain't Got Time to Die"

REMEDY

In that small place with the tin roof, I sat and looked deeply into my great-grandmother's cataract-covered eyes before asking her to tell me about him. I had heard that her father was a healer, and I wanted to know more. My great-grand-mother's name was Mae, but everybody called her Remedy.

After a long and warm welcome, Remedy turned up the heat. We settled in and she told me the story of a man who traveled the countryside laying his brown, calloused hands on those who were ill, helping them to see life again. Remedy told me of how he would gather her and her seven brothers and sisters and walk them into the woods. They would amble over sticks and rocks and snakes hiding in holes, to select only the tenderest of leaf, the sturdiest of root, or the most suc-culent of berry to take home to make his poultice. I tried to get her to remember what those roots were, for Remedy was a healer in her own right. When she was young, Remedy traveled from the country to live in the city, and the people in her urban dwelling would bring their children to her, she said, so that she could lay her brown, calloused hands on them and help them to see life again.

So I asked Remedy, "What was it that you used? Could you remember the root, the berry, the tender leaf?" For of course, it was the poultice, the medicine that

111

caused the healing. But Remedy had a different perspective. To her the doctor was God.

He's the Great Physician, he's my Lord.

—Anon, "He's the Lily of the Valley"

See, my daddy had the gift of healing. My mamma, too. And then I learned from them. Everybody in the community would bring their children to me when they would get sick, and I would make up some tea and things to make them all well.

My daddy would sit down and make these remedies, and we learned how he made them. When that flu was going around, people were dying by the dozens. Whole families died off. But my daddy, he stayed up and gave us some teas that he made, and we all got up and got well.

We would go out and make teas out of hole hollow root that you found in the woods and rabbit tobacco. Rabbit tobacco is good for colds, and it is good for your body. If you had a head cold, you could light a fire up under the leaf and put something over your head and breathe in the smoke. It would open your head up. It is real good. You know, children used to get that rabbit tobacco and smoke it. When the boys got big enough to think that they were little men, they would smoke it. They thought that they were taking a smoke, but they were taking some good medicine.

See, we lived about ten miles from town, and there wasn't much doctors around. We didn't know what it was to go to a doctor. We used to go in the woods and get all of this stuff. We didn't have to go to town to buy it. All of these different herbs were all out there. God has got all of the medicine in the woods to heal a nation. Us old peoples knows about that.

That is the reason that I am living so long. I was ninety-three years old in January. We didn't eat all kinds of food. We got fresh water and all kinds of fresh foods because we would raise them. We had well water and spring water. But now, ain't none of that pure. Man has done messed up God's gift to the world.

Peoples used to live way in the country and didn't know what it was to go to a doctor. I haven't been in a hospital. 'Cause I have a doctor I go to. Doctor Jesus. Don't leave him out. Sometimes you can't see your way through, and before you know anything else the door is open.

When people's children would get sick, they would bring them to me. My mind is getting kinda old, where I can't remember everything. But I do know this; we used to be our own doctor, us and Dr. Jesus.

I'd wondered why Remedy never got her cataracts fixed. I'd told her on several occasions that cataracts were an easily treatable condition. But Remedy would rather watch her sight slip away than go to a doctor—a human doctor, that is.

I knew through the stories shared on quiet summer afternoons that Remedy's father died of an equally treatable condition because the town doctor, whose hands were neither brown nor calloused, refused to treat "Negroes." I'd heard about toil's wracking pain and the sting of the lash that caused my ancestors to not want to give their bodies over. My elders told me of the meager wages that forced them to seek not only herbs but sustenance from that which grew freely from the ground. But until now, I thought that seeking God for healing was an alternative based on fear from the horrors previously mentioned rather than faith.

Months after talking with Remedy, I found myself in a surgical suite, surrounded by a team led by one of the most lauded physicians in my school. (Yes, I did return to medical school.) Like them, I stood sterilely while the doctor's white-gloved hand tenderly cradled the knife before puncturing the patient's brown skin. The blood rose. I later peered into a deep and gaping wound that the doctor made for healing and saw the throbbing of the patient's heart. Time was paralyzed. Slowly, I lifted my white-gloved hand, now splattered red with blood, and rested it in that warm and open wound. As gently as an ambling caterpillar, the inside of his body moved against my fingers. Within me, awe abounded. Above me, as the doctor gave instructions and the team scurried, a light shined softly and brightly. It was then that I understood Remedy's words. For truly even in this sterile space, the doctor was God.

a.a., *Redemption*, 1999. Acrylic on canvas, 11 x 14 in.

I believe I'll go back home,
I believe I'll go back home,
I believe I'll go back home,
An' acknowledge I done wrong.

When I was in my Father's house,
I was well supplied;
I made a mistake in doin' well,
An' now I'm dissatisfied.

When I was in my Father's house,
I had peace all the time;
But when I left home and went astray,
I had to feed the swine.

When the prodigal son first left home,
He was feelin' happy and gay;
But he soon found out a riotous life
Was more than he could pay.

When I was in my Father's house,
I had bread enough to spare;
But now I am naked and hungry, too,
An' I'm ashamed to go back there.

When I left home I was in royal robes,
An' sumptuously fed;
But I soon got ragged an' hungry, too,
An' I'm ashamed to go back there.

When I get home I'll confess my sins,
And my father's love embrace;
I'm no more worthy to be called thy son,
I'll seek a servant's place.

When his father saw him comin',
He met him with a smile;
He threw his arms around him . . .
"Here comes my lovin' child!"
He spake unto his servants—
"Go kill the fattened calf;
"An' call my friends and neighbors,
"My son has come at last!"

    —Anon, "I Believe I'll Go Back Home"

Redemption

She used to talk about his religious fervor and evangelizing as if they were symptoms of some dreadful plague. But we were fully preteens then, and how else was one to talk about a father? Besides, we knew nothing then of the wide rivers that he had crossed.

She was my closest friend, and that made him nearly family. The first time that I met Redemption, I was twelve and standing near him; I felt even younger. Whether it was the many pounds spread across his six-foot-four frame or the unmistakable command of his presence that caused the dwarfing in me, I am not quite sure. But small indeed I felt, and all the while inexplicably loved.

Thirteen years later, we sat in that familiar space that we called "the family room." I felt honored to be the listener. It was as if he was in some way sharing with me the most precious fruit of his harvest. The years had changed him some. His hair was a little grayer, his belly a little wider, but his eyes were as ever bright as they'd always been and his presence just as strong.

We began to pray. I offered gratitude for the sacredness of this moment. He, with a humility revealed only before the face of God, asked for a strengthening of his remembrance. Then Redemption told his story.

The type of home that I was brought up in was basically a Christian home. The only people that were around me were strong people that went to church regularly. So it was mandatory that I went. Our teachings were very limited, but they were believed and acted upon. We believed in God. We believed in Jesus, and we knew that if we got into trouble that the place to turn to was God.

When I was seventeen and out of high school, I went directly from my home in Columbia, South Carolina, to Indianapolis to work with my uncle. When I went to Indianapolis, God saved me. What that means is that, in my heart, I understood that when you live for God all of the things of the world, as far as drinking and smoking and gambling, all of these things are not what you are supposed to do. You are supposed to live according to the Bible. Because when you live for God, God is your blessing. You don't have to try to get your own blessing. All of these things I learned while I was in Indianapolis.

At that time, in Indianapolis in 1966, I made over ten thousand dollars. That was a lot of money during that time. I was working twelve and thirteen hours a day for the railroad. I worked with my uncle when I had time on Saturdays. He owned four family flats. My goal was to buy me a flat of my own and rent it out. That is what I was working hard and saving all of my money for. That was my goal. I was in the church and doing well in the church, and boom, I got drafted. I was drafted in 1969. I was nineteen years old.

When I got drafted, being a young person I didn't understand why I would have to go off to the service. When you are young in the Lord, you don't know all of the scriptures. You don't understand all of the reasoning of things. At first

I thought that God was working a miracle. When I went to report, they said that they couldn't find any of my records, and I was like, "Oh, thank you, God. I am not going to have to go!"

They sent me home and told me to come back that Monday. That Monday, they shipped me to Kentucky. I didn't even get a chance to say good-bye to my family. Being a young Christian, I just didn't understand what God was doing. On that misunderstanding, I slipped away from God.

Mind now brother how you step on the cross,
Your foot might slip and your soul get lost.

—Anon, "I Feel Like My Time Ain't Long"

In June 1967, I went to Vietnam.

I was a member of the first infantry division. My first evening there, they sent me out on ambush. While we were out in the woods walking in our ambush formation, I heard something that sounded like a rooster crowing. I said to myself, "What is a rooster doing out in the woods?" All of a sudden, I heard the rounds of bullets. I didn't know that the cock's call was a Vietnamese signal. I could only hear gunshots and see these tracers flying through the air. I hit the dirt as fast as I could and stayed there until it was quiet. That was my welcome to Vietnam.

By 1968, we had lost many of our men. I had been promoted to platoon sergeant. As platoon sergeant, I was responsible for all four squads. They say that we killed many Vietnamese, but we never saw them. Most of the Vietnamese were dragged away before we could do a body count. You would be in a big fire fight, and afterward you go out and look around and see only two or three people on the ground dead. The Vietnamese would have dragged all of their bodies off. It kind of messes with your head because so much is going on and so many rounds and so much artillery have been fired and you don't have any evidence of your success. It was mind boggling. That is what guerilla warfare does. When they fight you guerilla-warfare style, they work with your mind.

God was protecting me all of the time. I am saying this because I never got wounded while I was over there. It was the protection of God and the prayers of my family that allowed me to never get wounded. There were so many things happening around me. People got wounded. People died. People died and got wounded. Different things were happening, but God protected me.

When I got some time out of the field, I would drink this Vietnamese liquor called Silver Fox. One night I drank a pint of Silver Fox, and I passed out on the bed with this cigarette in my hand. When I woke up, the bed had caught on fire. The mattress was flickering red, and the fire was outlining my body. It burned everything but me. God protected me in that.

I stayed out in the bush a long time fighting in the jungles. I've seen big monsters in the jungle. We would have to pull our pants down after we walked through the waters because there were leeches all over us. We walked so long. I got through that year by the prayers of friends and by the grace of God. God brought me back to the United States. All of me. I came back in July 1969. When I got off of the plane, I kissed the ground. I was just so glad to be home.

O, sinner now is your time.

What you going to do when your lamp burns down?

—Anon, "What You Going to Do When Your Lamp Burns Down?"

When I came back home to my little town in South Carolina, I was in a back-sliding condition. When you come out of a situation like Vietnam, you are not the same person that left. My mind-set, the way that I carried myself, had changed. I began to drink more. I stayed out all night. I would stay with my old girlfriend from high school and run around with different women. I drank and partied and let it all loose. I got into altercations with the law. I was worrying my mother so much.

I was supposed to marry my girlfriend, but I didn't want to marry anybody. So I told her, "I am going to buy the ring in the morning." Then I got on the bus and went to Charleston. I wasn't in no mind for marriage. That is how I came to Charleston, not to worry my mother and not to marry that girl.

I came to Charleston and got into the fast lane. I was partying and having a good time, until I got hooked. Until I got so involved that I didn't have any control because everything was controlling me.

In 1969, I got a job on the river. By then my dreams of saving my money and buying the flats had vanished. I just wanted a nice car and to be in the streets and party.

I had a problem dealing with people when I got back because we had built a togetherness in Vietnam. When you are in a life or death situation, you have a togetherness. When I got back to the States and the blacks were not together, it disturbed me. I stayed angry all of the time. By then I wasn't even thinking about God. So I stayed angry and frustrated. The people in the shipyard knew it. I wouldn't associate with whites other than to do what I was supposed to do at my job. Except for this one white guy. I would talk to him because he could get the best marijuana. Sometimes he would give me THC. He was all right. But my anger was there.

So I worked in the shipyard, but in the process I sold marijuana. I sold Black Beauty. I used to gamble quite a bit and smoke a lot of marijuana. I smoked a lot of hashish and I smoked a lot of opium and drank extreme amounts. In the process of all of this, I had trouble.

I lived that life in Charleston for fourteen years. During those fourteen years, I got married and my children were born. Then I got divorced from their mother. The divorce was traumatizing for me, especially from the point of losing my children. I missed them more than anything else. Now mind you, during this time I was still drinking and doing drugs and living the fast life. After the divorce, I continued to drink until I became an alcoholic. It was to the point where whatever I could get high off of I would use it. I had come to that. Sometimes I would snort cocaine, if I could afford it. I thank God that at that time, crack was not in the particular circle that I was in, because no doubt I would have tried it.

This period lasted for about five years, and I couldn't do anything about it. I was functioning in the sense that I was working, but as soon as I got off of work, before I went to work, and during work, I would smoke marijuana. Or during lunch, I would drink a pint of liquor.

I realized that I had a problem when my sister and I went out to dinner one night with my second wife. I had been drinking. I was very loud and belligerent that night, and my sister, who is probably the closest person to me, walked off and said that she was never going anywhere with me again.

Afterward, I went out to the dumpster and I threw the bottle in that dumpster and I said that I was never going to drink any more. I tried to stop on my own, but the next morning when the liquor store was open I was right there buying another bottle. I had no control to control this thing myself.

That is why I understand when I see people who have gotten hooked. A lot of times, they want off, but they have no control. That is what the bondages of Satan do, using alcohol and drugs.

God's gonna trouble the water.

—Anon, "Wade in the Water"

My children would be here and there, and that bothered me. One particular time, my baby girl saw me, and she came running across a busy street to get to me. My son, I couldn't even find him. We had to walk all over the apartment complex to find him, and that bothered me. Every day I would say, "I am not going to drink this beer." But I couldn't stop. I would find myself saying, "I am going to stop drinking at twelve o'clock," and at 1:30, I was still holding a drink in my hand. I had no control, and all of these things were piling up on me. It was dealing with my mind, and I didn't know what to do. I didn't like myself any more. I didn't like what I had become. All of these things came to a head.

One night, I had been drinking and everything. I was at home and the frustration had built up so that I went upstairs and started picking up the furniture and throwing it down the steps. My wife left. When I got up the next morning and I looked around and looked at the mess, I just picked up the bottle to pour me a drink. I was going to get high so that I wouldn't have to deal with reality. I turned on the television with a bottle of rum in my hands, and as I was flipping through the channels I turned to a religious station. This guy was singing a song. To this day, I don't know what song he was singing, but whatever it was it seemed to bring everything about the Lord back to my remembrance. I put the drink down and I started crying and I started crying out to the Lord. I said, "Lord, save me. I don't want to live the life I am living. I don't want to be like I am. I don't want my children to be living like they are living." And I just began to cry out to God. I began to repent and I asked him to forgive me for everything that I had done. Everything that I could think of that I could repent of, I asked for his forgiveness. I asked for him to come in and cover me and change me because I didn't want to be like that no more. That was the morning that the Lord saved me and changed me. I wasn't in church. I was in an apartment.

The moment I walked away from those drugs, I had no appetite. I couldn't eat. So I just laid in the bed in a fetal position. I stayed in that bed for two days. I couldn't eat anything because all of that alcohol and stuff was having its effect on my body as it was coming out of my system. For two days, I was locked in that position with chills and body pains. After those two days, I got up and I was all right. That day God took the alcohol, the cigarettes, the opium, and the hash away. I never touched any of that again. That was seventeen years ago. I never touched any of that again.

Who that yonder dressed in green?
Look like the member that been redeem.

— Anon, "Go, Mary, and Toll the Bell"

The first thing that hit my mind was to go and look for a church. I stopped going around with my old friends. Afterward one of my running buddies came up to me in a car smoking a joint, and I told him, "Hey man, I ain't about that no more." I had to do that with all of my friends. I had to separate myself. At the shipyard, I got up and I testified to all of the guys who wanted me to go out with them for liquor. I told them, in that same place, I told them, "I don't do that no more. I am saved now." I said it in front of everybody. I separated myself from them and began to go to church.

In the meantime, one Friday night I came home, and I got on my knees and I said, "Lord, if it is better for my children that they be with their mother, keep them with her. But if it is better for them to be with us, then let them be with us." That was the prayer I prayed, and a month after that, they were here in our home. Not too long after, God blessed us with a house.

I would like to say that today their mother lives a great life. She is a precious lady and a good and loving mother. Her life has changed also. My kids are good kids, and the reason that they are the way they are today is because of some of the things that she put in them. But at the time, there was a struggle in her life, and I wasn't satisfied with what was happening with my children. So I just prayed.

My children, my wife, and I began to go to church, and for two years, we have five services a week at this church, me and my family didn't miss a service at that church. I just didn't want to go back into the world.

> *I believe I'll go back home.*
>
>   —Anon, "I Believe I'll Go Back Home"

In 1985, I went to Detroit and I fasted for seven days. In the midst of that, I asked God, "God, why did I blackslide?" And God said, Romans 8:28: "We know that all things work together for good for those who love God, who are called according to his purpose." If I had had this scripture in my spirit then, I wouldn't have backslid because I would have known that all of the things that were happening would have worked for my good, if I keep myself connected with him.

In this day in time, I have been called into the ministry. I preach the Word now. I have been preaching for about five years. We have a ministry at our church where we work with the drug pushers. We go out to all of the housing projects, and we hold street meetings and rallies, and we push the Word. People that have been hooked on crack are being saved. They are being set free and delivered. We have people in our church who were crack addicts and are now playing instruments and praising the Lord.

I just want people to know that if they let their heart speak and ask God to come in and change them, then he will do that because he is God.

I gave him a long hug before saying good-bye. Though close to thirty, I still felt like less than twelve in his arms and inexplicably loved. When my friend opens this book and realizes that she is reading her father's words, I have no doubt that she will turn the pages slowly. Her lips will likely curl, as they always do when she tries to pretend that she is not moved, and her heart for him, stretched through the wear of years, will widen. She will probably call me then. Beyond our initial joking, I will hear the tears in her voice and will be able to envision the shine in her eye. There will be probably be a moment of comfortable silence before we begin. For again, my friend and I will be surely be sharing a sentiment as we talk of Redemption. But this time, the sentiment will be pride.

a.a., *Faith*, 1998. Acrylic on canvas, 8 x 10 in.

*L*et us break bread together on our knees.
Let us break bread together on our knees.
When I fall on my knees, with my face to the rising sun,
Oh Lord, have mercy on me.

Let us drink wine together on our knees.
Let us drink wine together on our knees.
When I fall on my knees, with my face to the rising sun,
Oh Lord, have mercy on me.

Let us praise God together on our knees.
Let us praise God together on our knees.
When I fall on my knees, with my face to the rising sun,
Oh Lord, have mercy on me.

—Anon, "Let Us Break Bread Together"

D O C

He stood there regally, draped in African Mudd Cloth, somewhat of an anomaly in this store that served smoothies. It was a busy day and hot. The air was thick as only Atlanta's red clay could bake it. And I, minutes past the end of my shift, was tired. I wanted to leave early that humid afternoon, but my relief was late. Had it not been for her characteristic tardiness, I may have missed him.

"Dr. Muldrow. Lycurgus Muldrow," he said when I asked him his name. He looked nothing like any doctor I'd ever visited or studied with, but I believed him. It wasn't his clothes, for Afrocentricity was "in" and living in the Black Mecca as Atlanta was so astutely called, I'd seen my fair share of African regalia. It was his face that moved me. It radiated a peace and warmth that I had seen only on occasion in selected church elders. He stood there, regally, in cloths of Mudd and must have sensed the quizzicality behind my stare. For he paused a moment before smiling and said, " I am a spiritual healer." And I believed him.

Healing water over in Jordan, how I long to see that day.

—Anon, "Gideon's Bank"

133

We were at the Coumba Lamba ceremony, which was a nine-day ceremony in Saint Helena, South Carolina. They brought a group of African healers to America to do a traditional healing ceremony called the Coumba Lamba. They also brought Native American spiritual healers from throughout the United States to welcome the Africans to this land.

People from all over the United States came. It was probably nine hundred people there, and the healers were continuously seeing people during the nine days. At one point, one of the participants came to me and said, "I am amazed with all of the miracles that are going on!" I said, "Yeah, what are they?" And then she started mentioning all of these people that had been seen by the healers and how they had been healed.

After she told me that, I said, "Okay. Now where are the miracles?" She looked at me sort of perplexed and said, "Those things that I just told you! The healings are miracles." I looked back at her and said, "Oh, that. That happens all of the time."

I said this to say that there are no difficult healings. It is just a state of mind. It does happen all of the time, and when you see them as everyday occurrences and not miracles then it can happen to you.

Had he told me this story five months earlier, I probably would have thought him evasive. But now, I had heard the stories of seven who had made it to the other side. I'd seen the stamp of victory across their brow and noticed somewhat of a brow change of my own.

He invited me to a ceremony, a healing ceremony, at his home. As I parked my car, the drum beat beckoned. I opened his unlocked door, and above the curling smoke rose the voice of a woman with the gift of calling the ancestors forth. Before I was invited in, she sternly placed white clay on my forehead. "For protection," she said. Libations were poured.

There were ten of us there that afternoon. We sang and wailed. We danced and embraced. It seemed like hours passed. As the drums' calls lessened and the smoke cleared, a beautiful one, middle aged but with the aura of an elder, looked deep into my eyes and said, "You, my daughter, are nearing the close of a divine and healing journey." And I believed her.

a.a., *Akanke*, 2000. Acrylic on canvas, 4 x 6 in.

I will overcome
I will overcome
I will overcome, someday.
Down in my heart,
I do believe
I will overcome someday.

—Anon, "I Will Overcome"

AKANKE

She was beautiful. I walked into the restaurant and noticed her sitting there with her hair wrapped in kente. Her face was flawless and illuminated by joy's inner light. For at least fifteen minutes, I waited. I'd come to meet Akanke, a woman who had been disfigured in an accident. I heard about Akanke through a lady I'd met once at a conference. And though we'd never seen each other, Akanke and I had spoken several times. I imagined her to be scarred, wheelchair bound, and somewhat reticent. So when the beauty-filled one approached me kindly and asked if I were Alita, I was surprised. She afterward smiled broadly and said sweetly, "Alita, I am Akanke." Bashfully, I rose to give her my embrace.

Akanke saw me walk in fifteen minutes earlier, but I also was not as she imagined. She thought that I would be a woman older and sterner, with a face full of answers rather than questions. We laughed a bit before ordering. Akanke then began her story. That afternoon, I realized that appearances aren't actuality at all.

In May I graduated from phlebotomy school. I was an honor student. In October I was working with a girl in phlebotomy at Arizona State. That afternoon, she kept telling me to be careful. She said, "Be careful." I, on my way home, passed by the hospital and ended up there that night.

It was October 8, 1993. I was riding bus number 35 on Acorn Drive, and the driver dropped me off on an island at the intersection of Acorn and Maple. I don't remember anything after that. A man ran a red light, and he hit my body into another car. I was crushed between both cars. The policeman was going to write the report because they thought that I was dead at the scene. But the paramedics felt my pulse. So they sent me to the hospital. I was in a coma for two weeks in an eight-unit ward. I was twenty years old at the time.

They thought that I was going to die. I was hemorrhaging from the brain down. My pelvic bone was hanging out of my vagina. My ankle was dislocated, my jaw was dislocated, and my eyes were poked out of their sockets. People were dying next to me, but I faced death. I faced death while I was in that coma. It was a spirit of peace in me, and I didn't feel any pain. All I could feel was the spirit that I was going to make it. It was like I was on a cloud somewhere. I was on a different spiritual level. I didn't remember the pain.

So when I woke up, I was in a new world. I really was hurt. My face was disfigured, and they said that I would never walk again.

> *When the doctor, the doctor done give me over,*
> *King Jesus is my only friend.*
>
> —Anon, "King Jesus Is My Only Friend"

I stayed at the hospital in Arizona for a month before they would let me go back home to Denver for rehabilitation. When I went to Denver, I was in a wheel-chair. At the time, I was thinking, "Why me?" I was going through a depression state when I was in the wheelchair. People would look at me and point at me. Some days, I just sat there and cried. I couldn't deal with myself in that wheel-chair, and I was mad at my body. Faith in the creator brought me out of the depression. I come from a background of very strong spirits. Sometimes there is a reason to slow you down. There is a purpose. You must know who is in charge. Sometimes trouble is there to awaken you and let you know that it is time to come on a higher spiritual level. You have grown out of one plane, and it is time for you to advance to another.

They told me that I was going to be paralyzed for life. When they told me that, I said, "I rebuke it. All things are possible with the creator. You are not God." I started walking three months later.

They told me that I could never be a phlebotomist or a nurse. They say that there is not hope for anybody with head injuries. I am still disabled, and I am also a nursing student. I have an A average out of my courses.

They are trying to figure out, "How can Akanke do that?" I say, " I rebuke it because only the creator knows what I can do."

There are all types of disabilities. Stevie Wonder is blind. Bill Cosby's son had dyslexia, and that didn't stop them from their dreams and goals. I know a man with no hands that builds computers. How can somebody label you? They are not God. Only God knows our possibilities.

I am a soldier. I am a warrior. I am a conqueror. I was taught that in my upbringing. So I rise. I am going for nursing even though they discourage me. I will get that degree. I tell people, don't let nobody, no enemy come toward you and say that you can't. Don't believe it 'cause you can do anything.

It's my determination to hold out to the end.

         —Anon, "Hold Out to the End"

I have been through a cycle of all types of things. I can go on and on. Before the accident, I had been a battered wife, and I had lost babies, but I am not going to get into all of that because my purpose in life is to be determined. I will stay prayed up because you have to fight the power every day. You have to have that positive energy to stand strong in your beliefs. You must focus. Be a doer.

I tell people to always give thanks to the creator and submit to him. Read and meditate. Pray and fast. Always, always focus on positivity, because negative energy will keep you down.

I still go through trials and tribulations. It isn't always easy. Many times I dreamt that that car was still on me. But I have to keep myself humble to the creator and not let the enemies fight within me. I will not let them keep me down. I have to encourage myself and pray and meditate within myself. I have to continue to tell myself, "I am somebody. I can do this." Sometimes it takes time to overcome something, but now I am overrunning it.

You told me to pray and I done that too.
I prayed and prayed till I came through.

         —Anon, "Good Lord, I Done Done"

It was painful, hurtful, and surprising. Getting to the other side was hell. I am still going through things now, but I am not going to bow to ignorance. I am constantly going, moving forward. I keep the faith. I keep growing because I have a son, and I can't just give up. I just can't give up.

My purpose is to teach people, to tell my testimony and encourage and heal people. I have a hand out for people who are in the midst of sickness and difficulties. I have a hand out to guide them. I have the experience to tell them how to overcome things—and then start to overrun things. There was a reason that the creator got me here—to fulfill his purpose. He hasn't finished with me yet.

When we left that afternoon, the day was sunny, and Akanke walked slowly and proud. Encouraged by this encounter, I, on the way home, thought about the fallacy of appearances, the limits of our sight. The event that disfigured Akanke in actuality made her beautiful. That which disabled her made her strong. I thought about my own journey and the struggles that I had to take this year, for I thought that in this decision I had forsaken my future, my career. In reality, I was on the path to finding it. What appeared to be a rebuffing of medicine was in actuality a receiving of healing. And that afternoon, for his limitless sight and tender wisdom, I thanked God.

a.a., *Tony,* 2000. Oil on canvas, 8 x 10 in.

hy should I feel discouraged?
Why should the shadows fall?
Why should my heart be lonely,
And long for heaven and home?

When Jesus is my portion,
A constant friend is he.
His eye is on the sparrow.
I know he watches me.

I sing because I'm happy.
I sing because I'm free.
His eye is on the sparrow.
I know he watches me.

—Civilla D. Martin, 1905
"His Eye Is on the Sparrow"

TONY

I thought that Akanke's story would be the last. By now I had returned to medical school. I'd submitted the manuscript, and the publishing contract was signed. Though I was excited about the fact that others would be able to share in this journey, somewhere within me, it did not seem complete.

It was a quiet evening. I was pouring through notes taken on patients that I had seen during the day. That month, I was participating in my internal medicine rotation on the unit in our hospital that served the needs of patients with AIDS. The month had been hard. Seeing the despair on some of my patients' faces rendered me speechless. I desired to share words of comfort, but felt that I had nothing substantial to offer these ones who were so astutely facing death. While sitting on the floor that evening and sifting through piles of notes, I felt helpless, hopeless, and overwhelmed.

The phone rang, and I dug through scatterings of papers to grab the receiver. In the background, I heard the chiming of intravenous monitors and thought that it was the hospital calling about a patient or a task left undone. But the voice sounded like no nurse's. It was far too frail and spoke as if inhaling breath was a feat, priceless and prized. After ensuring that I was indeed the one that

he was seeking, the caller told me that his name was Tony. Tony had heard about
the book through a mutual friend and while lying in his hospital bed was moved
to call. He was in New York. I was in New Haven, and on top of the piles of scat-
tered papers, I set my tape recorder down. That evening over the telephone wires,
Tony testified.

Why should the shadows fall?

—Civilla D. Martin, "His Eye Is on the Sparrow"

Basically, this life really started when I graduated from high school and I moved to New York. I wanted to see the world, so I decided to venture off by coming to New York. When I got here, I was so excited by the flashy lights and the clubs and everything. I was pretty much apt for anything. I guess Satan found my weakness and decided that he wanted to do something with me. It didn't matter sexually if it was a man or if it was a woman that was thrown at me. I was ready. The first thing that came into my life was the first thing that I took heart to. Unfortunately, it happened to be a man. From that point forward, it went.

I was in a relationship for about ten years with one person. There were some good times, there were some bad times, but the good did override the bad. When I first met him, I had already been declared HIV positive. I knew that I had to set my own destiny. I knew that I was in control of my own life. I decided not to do counseling or the medications. I explained it to him and I told him the truth. I was very up front and honest with him. He was the one that stood by me those ten years. You know, anybody in their right mind probably would have ran away ten years ago when someone said that they were HIV positive. But for some reason, he didn't care. It didn't matter what I had; I guess he really cared about me.

I broke off the relationship about three years ago because I couldn't do it any more. Something just came over me and said, "Tony, this is not for you. This is not you. It is not worth the pain. It is not worth the suffering. It is not worth the insecurity and all of those things that you have to deal with in a relationship." So I was cut off from that.

I lived out my life to the point where my immune system got real low. It had gotten to the point where I had gotten real sick. I came down with pneumonia and thought that I was going to die. But with God's unchanging hand, he said this is not your time. We are going to give you another chance. So he brought me through that, and after I went through that I still hadn't changed my lifestyle. I still was doing what I was doing, and I was basically getting sicker and sicker by the minute. My feet were like water balloons. It was to the point where I couldn't even walk. I was in a wheelchair. I couldn't even drive my car. I had to get people to try to take me around.

I sing because I'm free.
> —Civilla D. Martin, "His Eye Is on the Sparrow"

So something came along. A person came along at the clinic in which I was attending. She came up and spoke some words to me. She had been there for quite some time, but I never noticed her. She knew me, but I never acknowledged her or anything. One day something just prompted me to speak to her. I spoke to her, and from that point we just started talking. Talking led to lunch, dinner, walks in the park, and that sort of thing. Then, she invited me to come to church with her. I went to Bible study with her one Tuesday, and the pastor gave a real powerful word. I have heard a lot of pastors preach, a lot of ministers, but there was something unique about this particular pastor. His words seemed like they were coming directly from God. You could tell that he was an anointed man of God. After the service was over, I grabbed my things, and as we were going out the pastor said, "Thanks for coming. I would like to see you back."

The following Sunday, I went to church. I went to hear him preach, and he gave another powerful sermon. Then it came to the point where he was like, "Is there anybody here that wants to rededicate their life to the Lord?" During this time, I was standing at my feet, and this young man, who had an anointed voice of God, was singing "His Eye Is on the Sparrow." Why did he sing that? I was pouring tears down from my eyes. I was standing at my chair, and the pastor said, "Come. This was for you. His eye is on the sparrow."

I went before the pastor and I stood before him. I cried. I cried. He grabbed me and he gave me a hug. He said, "Tony, God has spoken to me. He has told me that he has extended your life." I was like, this man doesn't know nothing about me. He didn't know that I have HIV. But he said, "God has extended your life. In the name of Jesus, you have been healed." It felt like an anointing came raining down on me. It was like something just went through my body, almost like I was getting an electrical shock. It was so powerful. I just knew. I felt the healing in my body, in my mind, and in my spirit. It felt miraculous.

Glory and honor, praise Jesus. Glory and honor, praise the lamb.

—Anon, "Praise the Lamb"

Afterward, the preacher said, "Tony, God wants you to be a testimony to other people. Tell them about him." Ever since then, God had been working wonders in all aspects of my life. I know what I have been through, and I can honestly say that God has healed me. My Lord Jesus Christ saved me. He said, "Tony, it is time for your healing to come about." And the way God works is not always the way you want him to, because he works in his own time. Even though you might want him to heal you today, he is not going to do it. He is going to do it when he feels that it is the right time. Therefore, you just have to be patient. I still have HIV, but I know that God has constantly and continually healed my body as the days go by. I can't move as fast or as swift as some people, but I am able to walk, and that is a blessing within itself.

God has taken a lot of desires and stuff away from me. I know that things really don't happen overnight. As I became saved, I was still a sinner, but God has also healed me and given me deliverance from lust—lusting men, lusting women, that sort of thing. I no longer have the desire to be with a man intimately any more. God took that taste out of my mouth, and now he has put a woman in my life that I love so much and she loves me. If we could get married today, we would. It is a wonderful thing how God just took the taste out of my mouth so fast. The only person that I know that can do that is him. I just pray that people will find it in their heart and their soul to turn to him and they will see the difference of what he will do for them.

Children, children give up your heart to God

—Anon, "The Rocks and the Mountains"

Through God I have gained great strength, knowledge, and wisdom. I am going to keep in his word, which will give me more strength to deal with life, the world that we live in, and the people that are here. There are so many different types of spirits that are out there that we come up against. But the Lord says that if you are on his side, he will always be present. He will always watch over you. He will always intercede in case something comes up. For you are his child.

God says that you are not ordinary. You are extraordinary. You are not ordinary, and don't ever let anybody tell you that you are ordinary. You are wonderful because God formed you. He made you. He formed you. I know that God has bestowed greatness upon me. He has bestowed extraordinary. Because when God made man, he made man great!. He didn't make him good. He made everything else good. But when it came to man, he made him great. That is what I feel. I feel as though I am great. And even though I may have been disobedient, God knows that I have always loved him. I was just apart, and it was time for me to come back home. I am so glad, and I really just thank him for my healing. Through all of the misery and all of the strife that I have had to endure in my life, I am so grateful to him because he said, "The race is not given to the swift or the strong, but to the one that has endured to the end." I am enduring until the end.

As much pain as Satan may afflict to my body physically, he can never touch me spiritually. I just thank the Lord for that. Satan knows that I belong to the Lord. I can go tomorrow or today, and I know that I am happy, because he has given me peace and joy and happiness in my life. I am not afraid. I do not fear death any more. Because God knows that I am his child and he has given me eternal life.

I've got a home on the other side.

—Anon, "Swing Down Chariot"

I want people to know that they need to have some type of spiritual well-being about themselves, and not just be lost out here in the world. They need some type of guidance. If they feel as though they don't have guidance, and they don't have meaning, the only person that can give them guidance and meaning is God. You have to go to the source. If you go to him, you won't be running around this world with your head cut off like a chicken. You won't be asking, "What is it that I am fighting for? What is it that I am living for? Am I living for prestige, power, money, or position?"

What is it that you are looking for in life? What is it that you are trying to get out of life? You have to go to him, and he will give you meaning. Read his word. He will let you know.

If people were to do that, then they will find out their purpose, because we weren't put here just to be here. Now out of ninety-nine million sperm cells, do you tell me that yours just happened to be the one that God chose? Believe me, you were not the only sperm up there fighting to get into that egg. Trust me. So you'd better know from that point that you are somebody special and that you are somebody wonderful and that you are extraordinary to be here. You are.

That was a great revelation for me. I look at that and I'm like, Tony, God chose you out of all of that. He picked you out of all of that to be here. I just thank him. As people return to him, they will find the healing within. There is one true and living God. You can go to his altar any time for guidance and healing. That is why I serve him.

I am just so thankful. I am so thankful for how God has changed my spirit. I just pray and hope that for all of man's eternity that they will finally come to a decision in their life of who is most important. Who is most important, and who will provide them with anything that they need. Whether it is materialistic, physical, or spiritual; if God gives it to them, he is the only one that can take it away.

The Lord has been my rock. He is my rock and salvation. He is my stronghold. He is my watchtower. He will not let any enemy come up against me. I know that in life there are trials and persecution, but now I am on God's side. I can tell you right now, God's right hand and holy armor will get you to victory.

Through the rivers of pain and insecurity, storms of isolation and anguish, and oceans of uncertainty and despair, these wonderful ones who were touched to speak about their journey found healing by crossing over into the arms of God. While still wet from wading, Tony stood that evening celebrating his passage, proclaiming his healing while looking squarely at the face of death.

One may think that this is the end. But the truth is that it is only the beginning. Through this healing journey, I have been led to a different path. For that evening, after hearing Tony's testimony, I knelt humbly and gave my heart to God. I, too, crossed over. And after weeping and giving thanks, my spirit smiled, for I knew that the other side would be my side evermore.

a.a., *Alita Emerging,* 1999. Acrylic on canvas, 8 x 10 in.

*A*s his people stood by the waterside,
At the command of God, it did divide.
And when they reached the other shore,
They sang a song of triumph o'er!

—Anon, "Go Down, Moses"